Also by Ruby Gwin

A Day That Would End Tearing at Your Heart

The 250th Field Artillery Men Remember World War II

RUBY GWIN

Also by Ruby Gwin: A Day That Would End Tearing at Your Heart

Order this book online at www.trafford.com
or email orders@trafford.com

Most Trafford titles are also available at major online book retailers.

Cover Design: Ruby Gwin

Book Design: Ruby Gwin

Picture is courtesy of Monte Bankhead and painted by author

Note for Librarians: A cataloguing record for this book is available from Library
and Archives Canada at www.collectionscanada.ca/amicus/index-e.html

Printed in Victoria, BC, Canada.

ISBN: 978-1-4251-4898-0 (sc)
ISBN: 978-1-4251-4899-7 (e-book)

*Our mission is to efficiently provide the world's finest, most comprehensive book publishing
service, enabling every author to experience success. To find out how to publish your book, your
way, and have it available worldwide, visit us online at www.trafford.com*

Trafford rev 10/19/2009

North America & international
toll-free: 1 888 232 4444 (USA & Canada)
phone: 250 383 6864 ♦ fax: 812 355 4082

THANKS

$\mathcal{T}$hanks to Dennis Weaver, son-in-law of Barney Howard who served with the 250th Service Battery, for this book was his idea. Dennis, too, served his country with distinction. He served not only with the United States Army for seven years, but spent 23 years as a Special Agent with the FBI. Dennis now helps John Walsh find missing children in the National Center for Missing & Exploited Children. What a résumé!

Thanks to each of you that participated—I myself, got a history lesson from all the via-telephone conversions....

DEDICATION

To the 250th Battalion's beloved Commander,
Lt. Colonel William K. Jealous,
Generals' Patton, Patch and LeClerc; Officers
and to all our 250th brave men
living or dead
who contributed to the success of the
U.S. Third & Seventh Armies.

Each man did his part—no matter the capacity.

CONTENTS

INTRODUCTION

*T*he start of the World War II was traditionally September 1939, when Nazi Germany invaded Poland. China had been at war with Japan for two years. France and Britain declared war on Germany—an ineffective gesture. In 1940, Germany invaded neutral Denmark and Norway to secure essential mineral supplies. Italy (aggressors) declared war on France and Britain. Germany was amply supplied with essential materials by the Soviet Union, which would concentrate on their own expansion. War between Germany and the Western Allies finally broke out *in earnest* in April 1940, eventually global by the end of 1941 after the Japanese attack on Pearl Harbor. The United States declared war on Japan on December 8, 1941, the very next day—it was D-Day in the Pacific.

The United States Army had a Selective Service Act (known as the draft) in 1940. In 1941, the age for military service was changed from 21 to 19 to increase military manpower. Many rushed to volunteer for U. S. Navy and Marine Corps that did not take conscript after the Pearl Harbor attack. The United States gathered its forces as never before to defend our shores and our freedom, fighting on two fronts at the same time.

United States was recovering from the Great Depression and still with memories of World War I that our soldier's would relive through Europe in World War II.

The Normandy invasion, the sheer size, scope and complexity of "Operation

Overload", was the code name for the horrendous events. The greatest invasion in history, acts of bravery, heroism or sacrifice made during World War II throughout the world.

The 250th Battalion had been chosen by General George C. Patton to serve with him and through that selection it gave the battalion the chance to serve under another elite' commander, General Alexander "Sandy" Patch. We were embarked on a two-front war, which promised to be a war of attrition. It wasn't a pleasant time; no war is. With being together so long—you became a family of brothers'—that still stands today! Each of you served under a most difficult task wearing the same uniform and performing to your maximum with—wings of a prayer.

Hunting souvenirs was rampant. Some got home with the prize—P-38 Lugar, but most of all, for each, it was hard to have to leave fallen brothers behind who so bravely gave their life. Like General McArthur said, "Old soldiers never die–they just fade away." The tales are fading; history has changed the image of the war that you brave men so nobly fought alongside of each other to the finish line. Veterans' contributions in history have been downplayed and ignored, from most textbooks. A war that was started when the Japanese bombed Pearl Harbor with their surprised attack on that early Sunday morning of December 7, 1941 killing thousands of our men, many would suffer from the global war and unbridled hatred. It is sad to try to vision what happened to the innocent people: women, little children and men who were killed and starved because of hatred.

Each of you had no great compulsion to relate your experience after you returned home. I want our grandchildren and great-grandchildren to know the true dedication, love, and the strong faith shown in that period of history. Your legacy is to be proud of, but it has been called into question in our grandchildren's history textbooks. I want them to receive a historically correct interpretation. I am sure that is why Dennis Weaver mentioned doing this book. We could solve some of today's problems that seem to grow bigger day by day if we would take a lesson from what you each gave. You taught us—you do not go alone as you fought for *freedom*. It takes *faith* and *truth* and *love* that were so bravely shown.

Your Commanders, Officers contributed immeasurably with *brilliant* leadership … all working *together* to defeat the enemies.

It is impossible to tell the story as those that were down there on the front lines. To describe day by day life experience of those who fought it out with sheer courage. Each of you came under your own personal observation which only you can convey to our children, grandchildren and lay readers. Many World War II veterans have been interviewed to try to recreate the singular psyche of your experience of the war for history … hopefully; it will be kept in tacked.

Relieved of military duties and homeward bound I pray each of you realized what you had given your country. It was a sacrifice so nobly given. They say— to raise a child it takes a village—just as war—it takes dedicated soldiers and superiors. Your stories give us a greater understanding for what you sacrificed and what the war conditions were really like. I hope you can appreciate how I admire all of you for your energies and talents. The 250th Battalion relished the time spent together. Words could never adequately express the strength and courage shown … God Bless!

Our 250th Battalion

They gave to keep us safe…
Through greed and hatred and fear,
They gave solely in our hours of danger.
Through "The Darkness" they led,
They gave "Thy Light" by wisdom.

Ruby Gwin

Major Ford P. Fuller, Jr., USA 1945 (top left)

Colonel Ford P. Fuller, Jr., USA 1961 (top right)

Colonel Ford P. Fuller, Jr., USA Ret. 2005
(bottom right)

Ford P. Fuller, Jr.

MAJOR, UNITED STATES ARMY S-3 OPERATIONS OFFICER
250TH FIELD ARTILLERY BATTALION—DECEMBER 1943–JUNE 1945

*B*orn November 26, 1917, in Savanna, Georgia, I graduated from Savannah High School in 1935. Entering the United States Military Academy at West Point, N.Y, in July 1936, I graduated as a 2nd Lieutenant in the Field Artillery in 1940. After a summer leave, curtailed because of the national emergency, I reported to Fort Sill, Oklahoma to attend the Officers' Basic Course at the Artillery School. As a matter of note, this was the last class to receive instruction in horse-drawn artillery as well as truck drawn artillery. After completion of this course late in 1940, I was assigned to the Division Artillery of the 4th Infantry Division (Motorized) at Fort Benning, Georgia where I served as a battery officer in a field artillery battalion armed at first with the French 75mm guns and later with 105mm howitzers. In early 1942, shortly after Pearl Harbor, the 4th Division was moved to Camp Gordon, near Augusta, GA to occupy the newly constructed camp and to continue its training.

In August 1942, as a Regular Army Officer, I received orders to report to Camp Maxey, Texas to be a member of a cadre of officers and non-commissioned officers for the activation and formation of the 251st Field Artillery Battalion. By that time, because of the war emergency, I had been promoted to 1st Lieutenant and then to Captain. For the next sixteen months or so, I was busy as the Assistant S-3, helping to train for combat the newly activated 251st Field Artillery Battalion. Our young soldiers, mostly from the states of Texas, Arkansas, Oklahoma and Louisiana, came in increments from basic training. With our sister unit, the 250th Field Artillery Battalion, we were a part of the 406th Field Artillery Group. Experiencing all the growing pains associated with a new unit, we moved along smoothly and within a year we were participating in Army maneuvers in Louisiana, taking Army Training Tests and proving to our superiors that we were ready for combat. The enlisted men who showed leadership ability were designated non-commissioned officers and those with technical and special skills given positions of responsibility and designated technicians. By December 1943, both the 250th and the 251st had passed their test with flying colors and were declared combat ready. At that time, within the 406th Field Artillery Group, some officer shuffling took place. As a temporary Major (and a Regular Army 1st LT.), I suddenly found myself transferred to the 250th Field Artillery Battalion. This came as a shock as I had been operations and training officer (S-3) of the 251st and knew intimately all the officers, key NCOs and many other enlisted men in whom I had the greatest confidence. Fortunately for me, both battalions had been well trained in basic field artillery fundamentals. My only difficulty in moving from S-3 of the 251st to S-3 of the 250th was saying farewell to one set of comrades and in acquiring a new set of equally qualified comrades.

Paris, Texas, the home of Camp Maxey, was a wonderful North Texas town. The people were warm friendly and opened their hearts and their homes to the large military contingent that eventually occupied Camp Maxey. The churches opened their doors to us, and the community went all out to welcome us and help us overcome our homesickness and our anxiety over what the future held for us. Over time, many of the local young ladies became engaged to, and some eventually married, men stationed at Camp Maxey. Since my heart was elsewhere when I arrived at Camp Maxey, I was not among those who married Paris girls. In January 1943, I managed to get a leave of one week to go to Savannah, GA, marry Peg and bring her back to Paris with me. Ever since, I have boasted that Peg and I spent the first year of our married life in Paris. And it was exactly a year, as we shipped out from Camp Shanks, NY on January 30, 1944, our anniversary, my parents' anniversary and the birthday of President Franklin D. Roosevelt.

By coincidence, my West Point classmate Michael F. Bavaro had the same job in the 250th that I had in the 251st. When I was transferred to the 251st, Mike, who ranked me several files, moved to the position of executive officer of the battalion or second in command. A big event in June of 1943 was the marriage at the Camp Maxey post chapel of Captain Michael F. Bavaro to Miss Janet Wagner, a charming young lady from Paris. I was Mike's best man in an impressive military wedding with attractive bridesmaids and groomsmen in Dress Blues who formed an arch of sabers for the couple as they left the chapel. In 1993, at Thousand Oaks, California, Peg and I helped Janet and Mike celebrate their 50th Wedding Anniversary with a large group of family and friends.

The reunion Group has done an outstanding job of getting us together after all these years and publishing the history of the 250th Field Artillery Battalion. Since World War II ended over 60 years ago, it would be foolish and futile for me to go into great detail over my memories of what happened from the time we sailed for England from New York to the inactivation of the 250th in June 1945. Therefore, with apologies to my 250th buddies who attended the reunion at Mountain Home, AR in 2000, I am taking the liberty to include in the next few paragraphs some notes of the talk I gave at that time.

CRYPTIC MEMORIES OF THE 250TH FIELD ARTILLERY BATTALION

August-September 1943, arrival at Camp Maxey of the cadre composed of officers and non-commissioned officers from units all over the country—assigning the cadre to key positions within the battalion; cadre training.

There was the arrival of troops from various basic training posts and specialized military school assignments. Assignment of troops was according to their training batteries: Headquarters, A, B, C, and Service. Comprising of obstacle course, 25 mile hike, unit training by section, unit training by battalion, battery tests, battalion tests, maneuvers in Louisiana. Return to Maxey to prepare for shipment overseas, arrival of overseas orders, sad farewells, departure of battalion for port embarkation, Camp Shanks, NY.

Memorable trip by train in January 1944 to Camp Shanks; loading in New York City of the battalion on British luxury liner converted to a troop ship. Unforgettable voyage in an Allied convoy through submarine infested waters of the North Atlantic from New York City to Liverpool, England. Traveling in convoy to Atherstone, Warwickshire in the Midlands of England to occupy a quonset camp set up on the estate of Sir William Dugdale. Meeting our English hosts; seeing a bit of England; trying to maintain our unit integrity while awaiting orders. Trying to communicate with our families by V-mail without breaking security and on June 6, was listening by radio to news of D-Day. Finally receiving orders (but not combat) to move by battery to various places in England to guard German prisoners captured in Normandy. Eventually receiving orders to reassemble and move to an artillery installation in Wales to brush up on our ability to move, shoot, and communicate. Officers and key non-commissioned officers while in Wales being assembled in an Army theater to hear General George S. Patton's famous *fight* speech. Moving to Southampton and loading on LST's (landing ship, troop), landing at Normandy with General Patton's Third Army, six weeks after D-Day, having taken longer to travel from England to France than from the U.S. to England.

Having as first assignment to reinforce the artillery fire of the French Second Armored Division, a combat experienced division of mostly North African troops and French officers, commanded by the well-known General Jacques LeClerc (nom de guerre). Our CO, Colonel Jealous, received orders from the Division Artillery commander to "Follow us." "To where?" asked Colonel Jealous. "A Paris (to Paris)," was the reply. Following those orders, giving support, as requested, from Normandy to Paris. On reaching Paris, for political reasons, being detached from the French and left in position on the outskirts while the French took two weeks to liberate the city and thereby experiencing our first disappointment of the war. Being reassigned to the French as they moved eastward towards Germany; being held down in a ready position with no action while our troops to the north successfully defended themselves, suffering many casualties but stopping and driving back the Germans in the Battle of the Bulge. Symbolically firing the first artillery round across the Rhine River into Germany, and supporting the fires of the French as they captured Strasbourg, France's easternmost city.

Being assigned to the 7th Army as it came up from its invasion of Southern France; reinforcing the fires of many divisional units of the XV Corps as we moved across Germany, winding up the war in a lovely little valley in Salzburg, Austria where we were enthusiastically welcomed by the Austrians as liberators.

Receiving good news and bad news; the good news that the war was over and we were being sent home. The bad news that the 250th was to be inactivated, and we were having to part company with our wartime buddies.

FINAL COMMENT

The efforts and the sacrifices of the 250th did not go unrecognized. All the divisions and the other units whose fires we supported looked forward to having the 250th assigned to them. On one occasion the Commanding General of the 100th Infantry Division was listening on his radio to the fire commands of his forward observers to the 250th. He called Colonel Jealous to say how astounded he was at the speed with which that "On the way" followed the forward observer's target locations. The Germans, who referred to the US fire as "automatic artillery", most certainly were referring to the 250th. And, of course, we are all proud of our Presidential Unit Citation.

We could not have done the job as we did it without the help and the efforts of everyone, cannoneer, cook, clerk, wireman radio operator, truck driver, mechanic, medic et al. We were a team and a darn good one! And we give our grateful thanks to those who got us back together in 1964. This team with its wives, children, and grandchildren has become a caring, patriotic organization, the 250th Field Artillery Battalion Family.

Every member of the 250th was, and still is, a hero. One of our members who are no longer with us was a special hero. Lest we forget, our leader Lt. Col. William K. Jealous had served in World War I and had remained in the Army

Reserve ever since. As the commanding officer of a small tactical unit such as the 250th, he was an old man, maybe 46-47 (somehow, that does not seem old now). When we slept in the open, ate out of mess kits and dived into foxholes, so did he. He was with us from the beginning to the end and he loved the 250th and everyone in it. So did his wife, Anita, whom we remember with great affection. They would be as proud of the 250th today as they were in 1945. As we remember all our departed members, their wives and their families, let us put Colonel and Mrs. Jealous at the head of our lists.

As an officer of the Regular Army, I did not return to the States until September 1945. I spent my leave in Savannah, Georgia becoming re-acquainted with my wife Peg, my parents, Peg's parents and meeting for the first time my 20 months old son, Ford III. I remained in the Army until my retirement in 1970 with the following assignments about each of which I could write a book:

1945–1949	Student/observer at the Escuela Superior de Guerra (War College) Mexico in Mexico City
1949–1950	Students Officers' Advanced Course, The Artillery School, Ft. Sill, OK
1950–1953	Assistant Professor of Military Science, The Virginia Military Institute, Lexington, Virginia. Promoted to Lt. Colonel
1953–1954	Student, Command and General Staff College, Fort Leavenworth, Kansas
1954–1955	Staff officer, Officer of the Secretary of the General Staff, 3rd Army, Fort MacPherson, GA
1955–1956	Commanding Officer, 49th Field Artillery Battalion, Korea
1956–1958	Staff officer, 1st Cavalry Division, Tokyo, Japan
1958–1962	Office of the Assistant Chief of Staff, Intelligence, Department of the Army – The Pentagon, Washington, D.C. Promoted to Colonel
1962–1966	Comptroller then G–1 (Personnel), Southern European task Force (SETAF), Verona, Italy
1966–1970	Professor of Military Science, Pennsylvania Military College (PMC), Chester, PA

Retiring in 1970, after 30 years of service, I lived in Delaware from 1970-1982. In 1982, we returned to Savannah, GA, our home town, living there until 1997. In 1997, we moved to Brandon Wilde, a life care facility in Evans, GA (near

Augusta). In August 2000, my beloved Peg died. We had been married 57 years. Our son Ford III lives in Pittsburgh, PA with his wife Kathy. Their sons are Ford IV (Chip) age 20 and John age 18. Our other son Middleton was born in Mexico. He resides in Palo Alto, CA with his wife Cheryl. Their sons are Thomas age 23 and Scott age 20. I still live at Brandon Wilde in Evans, GA, will be 88 in November 2005 and am in pretty good health.

First, I want to say, Col. Fuller's response to write the above story was one without reluctance. I found him not exploiting his "Colonel" title that he so *honorably* earned. Col. Fuller and classmate, Mike F. Bavaro at West Point, would both make Colonel. Col. Mike Bavaro is deceased.

I got to meet Colonel Fuller (Ford) for the first time, at his Georgia home in 2006. It is at the *top of the list of highlights of my life*. It was a trip I shall never forget. While we were there, Col. Fuller first called John Eberhardt and then Herbert Glazer. I personally got to enjoy a three-way conversation via-phone. It was a nice surprise. Just as Colonel Jealous, Colonel Fuller is the very essence of compassion, of duty, of style and of natural nobility who is classless.

I made it a mission to meet Col. Fuller; words cannot tell in part what it meant to me. Ford is a very captivating person that is enjoyed and *loved by all*.

Col. Fuller calling John "Jack" Eberhardt, (bottom), and a picture my husband, Carl, took of Col. Fuller and myself, (author), (top), just before our leaving. Carl and I left on a very hot, bright and sunny morning.

Colonel William Kingston Jealous

COLONEL WILLIAM KINGSCOTE JEALOUS

250TH FIELD ARTILLERY BATTALION

$\mathcal{C}$olonel Jealous was born 1894, in Pittsfield, Mass, where he attended various schools. He received a Chemistry degree from Worchester Polytechnic Institute in 1916. His "Army career" started when enlisted into the Army Reserves— history tells the rest. Holder of the Bronze Star with O.L.C.; Medal for Merit; Purple Heart; Croix de Guerre with a Bronze Star, Silver Star and Palm.

I chose to follow Col. Ford Fuller's story with this beautiful Eulogy Ford gave at a memorial service for Col. William Jealous & Anita Jealous. It tells of two people he knew, he loved and respected.

I first met Colonel William Jealous almost 41 years a go. As a young Captain, I was assigned to Camp Maxey, Texas to join a cadre of officers and non-commissioned officers to organize two field artillery battalions. Most of the senior officers of this group were Regular Army officers, but Colonel Jealous, then a Lt. Colonel, was a Reserve Officer. Having served in France in World War I, he had remained in the Reserve after his separation from the Service and had volunteered for active duty in 1940 as a result of the National Emergency.

We immediately began organizing, training and preparing for the arrival of our "fillers", the young soldiers, mostly inductees, who would make up our two units, the 250th and the 251st Field Artillery Battalions. Colonel Jealous was appointed the Commanding Officer of the 250th Field Artillery Battalion. By the end of that year, 1942, most of our men had arrived and had been assigned to the five batteries of the battalion.

For the next year we went through a vigorous training program to develop our two artillery battalions into combat units.

We were among the first occupants of Camp Maxey, an installation of newly-constructed, wooden temporary buildings located a few miles from Paris, Texas, a small town in the northeast part of the state. With 15 to 20,000 troops stationed at Camp Maxey, Paris, like most Army towns of those days, was taxed to the limit. Colonel and Mrs. Jealous, along with all the other married people of the command had to find their own quarters to rent in town. It was indeed a cultural shock for many of these people, particularly the younger newly-weds, to find themselves under wartime circumstances in Paris, Texas.

Colonel and Mrs. Jealous certainly rose to the occasion. They adapted themselves quickly to the situation, got to know many young officers and men and their wives and did a superb job of helping them to the new situation. At all times their home was open to everyone, and they took a paternal interest in the activities of the men, their wives and their families. During that year a great deal of camaraderie, love and affection developed between the Jealouses and all of their "children", as they called them, of the 250th.

Almost a year to the day after the arrival of the fillers, the 250th Field Artillery Battalion left Camp Maxey for the European Theater of Operations. Going by train to New York, and then by ship to Liverpool, England, we arrived at our final destination, Atherstone, England in January of 1944.

I had been transferred to the 250th from the 251st just a short while before we left Camp Maxey. So my acquaintance with Colonel Jealous had been more on a social, personal basis then a military one. It is remarkable, though, that because of the warm outgoing personalities of both Colonel Bill and Nita, my wife Peg and I knew them better than we knew any of the other senior people of the command. However, with all the problems incident to moving 500 men and their equipment halfway across the United States, across the Atlantic into a camp in the middle of England, it did not take me long to discover what a good soldier Colonel Jealous was. He was a gentleman through and through, dedicated to his job, easy to approach and readily adaptable to changing situations.

Let me give you a few highlights of the next year and a half we spent together. The people of Atherstone were very friendly. They invited many of us to their social functions, and Colonel Jealous and I frequently found ourselves at a week-end social or bridge game at the home of one of the local Atherstonians. With his military bearing, his New England air of formality, his courtesy, Colonel Jealous was very popular with our newly-acquired English friends. As a matter of fact, he and several others of us corresponded with a number of them for many years afterwards.

After about six months in England, our battalion was finally sent to France. It was the end of July, six weeks after the invasion of Normandy. Incidentally, since there was a lot of waiting time to offload reinforcements on that crowded beachhead, it took us longer to cross the English Channel than it had taken us to cross the Atlantic.

Naturally, we were apprehensive over our first assignment. Having been in France in World War I, Colonel Jealous was quite proficient in France. Therefore when we learned that we were to be attached to the 2nd French Armored Division, Colonel Jealous was in his element. He reported with great enthusiasm to Division Headquarters expecting a briefing and a formal field order as taught at our service schools. When he returned to our Command Post, however, he seemed a bit bewildered. When we asked him what our orders were, he said, "They told me, 'follow us'." "Where to?", he asked. "A Paree (to Paris)," was the answer.

Well, we had an interesting assignment with the French which I will not dwell upon. To our disappointment, for political reasons, we were not allowed to accompany the 2nd French Armored Division into Paris. As you might recall, the celebrations were so joyous that the 2nd Armored almost did not get out of Paris. We were then re-attached to them and supported them in the capture of Strasbourg in western France.

To make a long story short, the 250th ended the war in Salzburg, Austria where only a few days after VE Day the unit was inactivated and its men returned home.

As Battalion Operations Officer, I rode in the same command car with Colonel Jealous, bivouacked in the same place, shared the same rations and got to know him very well. Never one to take advantage of his position, Colonel Jealous lived as the rest of us, slept in a pup tent, ate out of mess kits and in general went through the same privations and discomforts as his men. The welfare of his men and their ability to meet their assigned tasks were always foremost in his mind. As a result, he was very popular with his men and the 250th was considered to be one of the best field artillery battalions in Europe, winning a Presidential Unit Citation.

After the war, Colonel Bill and Nita continued to keep up with their "children" who by then had children of their own. They visited us in Lexington, Virginia once in the early 1950's on one of their automobile trips between Maine and Florida.

Fortunately, the 250th had very little casualties in combat. Several years ago some former members of the 250th wrote the Department of the Army and got rosters of the old unit. They then formed the 250th Field Artillery Battalion Reunion Group which has had biennial reunions ever since. Colonel Bill and Anita attended these reunions while their health permitted. You can imagine the excitement and the enthusiasm which their presence created among the men and the women of the 250th most of whom are from Arkansas, Louisiana, Oklahoma, and Texas. They loved Colonel Bill and Nita, and they are all with us today in spirit.

Colonel William K. Jealous was a soldier. He served his country with honor and integrity in and between two world wars. As a fellow officer, a friend, an admirer and a representative of his beloved 250th Field Artillery Battalion, Colonel Jealous, I salute you and say, "Well done". And I salute Anita, his dear wife, whose heart went out to all members of the 250th and whose memory lives still in the hearts of all of us. May you both rest in peace.

Col. Jealous must have been a wonderful person. One can tell Col. Fuller truly respected and cared for both Col. William (Bill) Jealous and wife, Anita.

Anita and Col. Jealous

After entering Col. Fuller's beautiful Eulogy for Col. and Mrs. Jealous, I wrote the verse below. My meeting Col. Fuller and getting to know him, I found his Eulogy so profound that I felt a need to express it with an answer of what he means to those that have met him.

CAN'T IMAGINE

Her heart swells when she thinks of meeting him for the first time. With it, comes a complete memory of such friendliness, she holds his warmness inside her heart and finds it to be sacred; with a reminder how welcome he made her feel...

In reality, there is no end to her lifted feelings, and found she wanted to treasure her meeting this interesting and charismatic person...

She lifts her head toward the sky a-smiling; God heard her wish to meet this person of rank and made it come true, she *can't imagine* having never meeting him, for he is someone that leaves an imperishable memory in the heart of those that have met him.

Ruby M. Gwin

Colonel Jealous loved his 250th Battalion family. He wrote to clarify an error of their splendid record of accomplishments in this letter to Colonel Goddard in 1947.

West Southport, Maine
13 May 1947

Lt. Col. William B. Goddard
Hq. Third U.S. Army
APO 403. C/o PM, N.Y.

Dear Colonel Goddard:

I enclose the formal receipt for the "The Seventh United States Army, Report of Operations". It is a splendid and monumental work to have completed within such a short time. I am very happy to have it.

In the very cursory examination which I have thus far been able to give it, I find one error, viz., the report of the first American troops to enter Strasbourg. Vol, II, Page 436, 3rd paragraph reads in part:

"Although units of the 3rd Division entered Strasbourg.…..they were not the first American troops in the area. A special "T" Force had been organized for special operations in the city of Strasbourg.……"T" Force, including combat elements from the VI Corps, reached its destination by 25 November."

This credit should go to the 250th Field Artillery Battalion which I commanded. The facts, which are supported by my after action report for the month of November, are; I crossed the Vosges in support of Nassu via the Dabo road, (ibid pp. 410-1). On 23 November, in support of Rouvillois, I, together with my party, in the reconnaissance party of the Task Force, entered Strasbourg at 1030 hours the same day (ibid pp 416). By 1600 hours, my Battalion was in position along the canal through Schiltignen firing on the eastern end of the Kehl bridge. The first artillery of the Seventh Army to fire across the Rhine, possibly the first in the U.S. Army.

The events leading up to this action, while not germane to a history of the Seventh Army may be of passing interest. I was attached to the 2eme D.B. in the western outskirts of LeMans and reinforced the fires of their artillery, (the first truck drawn artillery to work with armor, so I have been informed) as far as and including Argentan. From there, with various U.S. Divisions I worked on up to support of the Mantes-Grassicourt bridgehead. The 2eme D.B. planned to pick me up there for their sweep to Paris. However, the XV Corps could not release me from that mission in time. I did not rejoin the French until I reached the Aube. At that time General, then Colonel De Langdale promised that my unit would be among the first into Strasbourg. When we reached the Vosges, he arranged with Colonel Crepain, 2eme D.B. Div. Arty., to have me attached to the Task Force which was expected to be the first to enter Strasbourg. That is the way he kept his promise.

In the interest of accuracy I thought that you would wish to have this correction. I shall be glad to have your comment.

Sincerely yours,
Wm. K. Jealous
Colonel, FA Res.

Major John S. Eberhardt at Schloss Glanegg near Salzburg, Austria—May 1945

John S. Eberhardt

During World War II, I was in a 105mm howitzer, truck drawn, and field artillery battalion. At various times, we were part of the corps artillery of three different corps, the Vth, VIth, and XVth, and, as corps artillery, we were assignable to any of the divisions within that corps, in order to supplement that division's regular, organic artillery. In this capacity, we fought with fifteen different divisions, and spent two hundred and ninety-seven days in combat without relief.

The corps artillery that we were most frequently a part of was in General Wade Haislip's XVth Corps, and the division to which we were most regularly assigned was the 2nd French Armored Division, commanded by General LeClerc, a French hero. This Division was composed of mostly officers from regular French army who had escaped to North Africa when their country had been taken over by the Nazis. There, they had been supplied with armored equipment by the Allies, and were veterans of the armored warfare in North Africa. Trained and experienced in armored tactics, they utilized to the fullest the elements of surprise and movement. When first assigned to them, we asked what our route of march and destination would be, and were advised, "We don't know. Just follow us!"

We were with this Division after the break-through at Saint Lo, when it spearheaded the drive of the Third Army to Argentan, and the famed closing of the Argentan-Falaise Gap to the German Sixth Army. We then went with them to Paris, where they liberated that city. During this time, we came to have the utmost confidence in them, and, therefore looked forward to being assigned to them. This was true, even though we were a truck drawn outfit, and, of course, all their organic artillery was armored.

In October of 1944, the Third Army offensive, after sweeping across France, bogged down about forty miles from the Vosges Mountains which extent northward into France from Switzerland, and form a barrier between the rest of France and the Alsace-Lorraine Valley bordering the Rhine. Static and bitter fighting continued through October, and the most of November. We spent this time assigned to an American infantry division, and suffered our worst casualties of the war.

During this period, I occasionally had access to the *LONDON CHRONICLE*, and other English newspapers which found their way forward to us. All of these papers had columns written by military analysts who made observations on possible, and probable, courses of action the fighting in Europe would take. I read these columns with interest, and particularly one written by a General Fuller for the *LONDON CHRONICLE*. I noted that he, and the other analysts, believed that it was well nigh impossible for the Allied Army to cross the steep and wooded Vosges Mountains, pointing out that neither side had attempted to cross these mountains during the First World War, nor, in fact, had any army in modern military history attempted it against a hostile force. It was their opinion that, due to the impregnable nature of these mountains, the Allied Army would be forced to move through the Vosges Gap, in order to reach the Alsace-Lorraine Valley on the other side of the mountains. The Vosges Gap is a valley some thirty or forty miles in width, which lies to the north of the Vosges Mountains. It was their conjecture that the Germans would naturally concentrate their forces in this gap, and that the Allies would encounter difficulty fighting their way through it. In fact, it was surmised that the fighting there could degenerate into World War I type trench warfare. This was a very unpleasant possibility to ponder.

In the meantime, and finally, after several weeks of fighting, somewhat like that of World War I, in which daily gains were measured in yards, a break through was achieved. At their request, we were again attached to the 2nd French Armored Division whose mission was to exploit the break-through.

As anticipated, we moved swiftly during the first day, and cut deeply into enemy territory. By evening, we were well within the enemy lines, and halted briefly for a meal of "C rations". When the order came to move out, our Battalion, as usual, found itself at the rear of the column. Our Battalion order of march was Headquarters Battery and then the gun batteries "A", "B" and "C" in that order, followed by Service Battery. At the time, I was in charge of the Battalion Fire Direction Center, and my command car brought up the rear of our Battalion, and hence the very rear of the entire column.

As we moved along, the Vosges Mountains began to loom ahead of us, dark and forbidding. I surmised that when we reached the foot of these mountains, our course would then turn northward along the base of them to the Gap.

The evening dusk turned to darkness, which was deepened by the dense woods which surrounded us and the complete blackout conditions under which we were of course traveling.

The column came to a halt. This was not unusual, and probably indicated that the head of the column had encountered some resistance, and I anticipated that we might be getting orders to go into firing positions. However, a short time later, the vehicles ahead of us began to move again. This did not last very long, and we again came to a halt. After a bit, I heard a vehicle approaching along the column. It was a jeep, and as it came up to my car. I recognized a lieutenant from "C" Battery, who was standing up in it with his hands clasped to the top of the windshield.

"We've lost the column, Captain!" He reported in an anguished voice.

In combat, that is something that one dreads even the thought of. To be lost! Especially if it happens to be behind enemy lines, as was now the case.

I dismounted from my car and got into his jeep. We turned around, and as we moved forward along the column, he related the details to me. It seems that one of the 2½ ton trucks pulling a howitzer in the middle of "C" Battery had bogged down. When they had it rolling again, the column was long gone. They tried to catch up with it, but had come to a fork in the road and didn't know which way to go.

Arriving at the fork in the road, I tried to determine by the only means at my disposal, the ground, in which direction the rest of the Division had gone. This proved to be impossible in the darkness, as both roads appeared to be well-used. I did not want to use my radio, as we usually maintained radio silence when operating behind enemy lines. For this reason, it also was extremely doubtful that I would receive any response, even if I did use it.

One road headed south, the other to the east. I could not conceive of any reason why we would be going south, and therefore, elected to take the road which went to the east, hoping that it would eventually turn toward the north and the Vosges Gap, which I imagined was our destination.

My command car with its occupants, the driver, the radio operator and the staff sergeant in charge of the Fire Direction detail, had now by-passed the column and were up with me. I remained in the jeep, however, with its driver and the Lieutenant.

I moved us out—one and one half batteries alone in the woods at night, and behind enemy lines. I kept hoping that the road would begin to turn toward the north, but it kept heading eastward. After a bit, we were climbing, and I had a sinking feeling in the pit of my stomach. There was now no doubt about it. "This must be the Vosges!" I thought.

There was no turning around. To the left of the road the ground dropped off sharply, and to the right there was a steep incline. There was, therefore, no alternative but to continue on, although with every passing moment the realization became clearer that we were indeed ascending the "impassable" Vosges Mountains. The words of the military analysts flashed through my mind, "Never in modern military history!", "Unthinkable!", "An impregnable obstacle!" Yet I was doing it with half of a gun battery and a service battery! Was I leading my small force to certain annihilation or capture? Had the main column taken the other road, the one to the south? These were the thoughts that entered my mind.

Presently, ahead of us loomed embrasures on both sides of the road with the muzzles of German anti-tanks peering over their tops and directed at the road in front of them. I halted the column and we moved forward in the jeep alone. Every moment we expected the flash of gun fire, but none came. We drew abreast of the embrasures, not knowing what would happen then. They were not manned! Yet there was no sign of any conflict. I reasoned that, if the main column had come this way, shouldn't these guns be knocked out? But then again, it was possible that the troops manning them might have been surprised and preferred to flee, rather than fight. Another possibility was that, not expecting that enemy troops were within miles of them, they might be off some place taking it easy. In any event, we in the jeep had a temporary feeling of relief.

I instructed the column to again move out, and we proceeded up the steep incline of the roadway. Further on, we again encountered more embrasures. Again I stopped the column and again we proceeded alone in the jeep. These embrasures were also unmanned, intact, and with no sign of any conflict.

On and on, higher and ever higher we climbed, until we eventually reached a small village of possible six or eight stone houses near the summit. There were no lights in the houses and no sign of life anywhere.

I halted the column. From here on we would be descending the mountains into the Alsace-Lorraine Valley. Before doing this, I decided that we should risk breaking radio silence in a final endeavor to make contact with the main column. I had my radio operator in the command car put out a call, but there was no response, just silence. We tried again. Silence. Again and again we tried, but with the same result.

I was pondering whether to push forward, or wait until dawn, when out of the darkness of the road ahead of us we heard the sound of a motor approaching. We were quite certain that it probably would be a German vehicle, and prepared ourselves for it. Instead, a jeep appeared out of the darkness and a French officer alighted and came forward. I went to meet him and we embraced. On his part, I guess this was from custom and delight on having found us. As for me, it was from sheer relief.

The main column had stopped about half-way down the mountain, and it was subsequently discovered that we were missing. At that point the French officer had been dispatched to try and find us. He led me and my small force down the mountain until we joined up with them. The amazing thing is, for a goodly number of the men and the officers of Service Battery, I don't believe they ever realized that we had been separated from the main body.

Apparently, the Germans had been taken completely by surprise, and had been away from their posts at the embrasures when the Division passed them. It was too late after that for them to put up any resistance, and they had remained hidden in the woods. It is lucky for my small force that they had remained there and not returned after the main column had passed.

At dawn, the Division descended the rest of the way down the mountain and into the Alsace-Lorraine valley. The Vosges had been crossed without the loss of a single man nor the firing of a single shot. It was evident of what quick movement and surprise could accomplish. Of course, we now found ourselves with a mountain between us and the nearest friendly support.

The French were able to plug into a German telephone line, and one of their officers who could speak the German language fluently warned them that a huge Allied force was approaching the Gap and to immediately rush as many troops as possible there. This ruse apparently worked, because the Germans did just that, and we were able to dash unresisted, some seventy miles across the Valley to the city of Strasbourg. This was accomplished in only two days. I imagine that the Germans responsible for defending the Vosges were too embarrassed at allowing us to slip through to report it to their High Command. I say this, because the Germans seemed to be completely unaware of our presence in the Valley for the first two days that we were there. In fact, when we rolled into Strasbourg on Thanksgiving Day morning, it was so unexpected that we surprised German officers out strolling on the sidewalk with their female acquaintances.

Strasbourg is, of course, located on the Rhine River across from Germany, and as soon as we were in that city, our gun batteries assumed firing positions with their guns directed across the Rhine into Germany. We set up our Fire Direction Center in one of the City's buildings and I realized that nobody in the War had, as yet, fired across the Rhine into Germany. I therefore quickly selected a target there, and gave the mission to "C" Battery, which Battery I had once commanded. We thus became the first unit to have done this.

We spent the rest of Thanksgiving Day in Strasbourg, but made an early departure the following morning before enemy troops could close in on us. We headed southward down the Valley to Colmar, and then turned and came back to the north following a different route. During this time we disrupted German communication lines, and our presence in their rear weakened their defense of the Valley.

After a few days, our mission had been completed, and we departed from the Valley over the mountains to the north of it.

Nearly two weeks after crossing the Vosges. I was interested to read in the STARS AND STRIPES (our Army newspaper) that the American VIth Corps had fought their way across the Vosges Mountains. They had accomplished this only after three days of bitter fighting, and after suffering an extremely high number of casualties. It was during this action that the well-publicized and valiant performance of the Japanese-American Brigade took place, and they lost almost half of their men.

About a week after that, the VI Corps entered Strasbourg and were credited with having liberated that City. They then sent one of their divisions southward, following almost the same route that we had taken earlier. In this instance, however, the enemy closed in on them and they had heavy losses, including one infantry battalion completely wiped out. Although we had fought some skirmishes, General LeClerc had kept us continually on the move, so that did not happen to us.

For some reason, American accounts of the War never mention the exploits of the 2nd French Armored Division. The fact that they were the first unit to reach the Argentan-Falaise Gap by a full day; their feat of crossing the Vosges, and their entry into Strasbourg, have gone unnoticed by American writers. Not so, I am sure, in French annals of the War.

In any event, that Division told us that, after all of the trials and tribulations we had experienced with them, they considered our 250th Battalion to be an integral part of their unit, and they gave us the privilege of wearing their prize "Cross of Lorraine" emblem. Due to our speed in delivering fire, General LeClerc always referred to us as his "Automatic Artillery".

Our Battalion was given a "Brigade Citation" by the French Government, which is their highest award to a foreign unit. Our exploits also did not go unnoticed by our own Government, and we were accorded a "Presidential Citation". That is the highest award the United States gives to any unit.

At Thanksgiving time a year later, and shortly after I had arrived back in this Country, I received a card from the mayor of Strasbourg commemorating our entry into his city a year earlier.

John would make Major—much deserved! John has a book he has written titled: "The Old Gray Mare". It may be ordered at Barnes and Noble Book Store. It is a must read!

John graduated from Princeton University and their ROTC Program. He was working for NBC Broadcasting Company before going into the Army. John (Jack) and wife, Elayne Avery Eberhardt, are so enjoyable to visit with by phone. They live in New Jersey.

Military wedding of Captain John Eberhardt C-Battery, 250th FABn & Elayne Avery at Camp Maxey,
Paris, Texas—April 11, 1943
Behind the groom and bride: Capt. Chester Philips and Louise Johnson.
Holding swords on left from door: -?-, 1st Lt. Herbert Glazer, 2nd Lt. Frank Roberson.
On the right from door: 2nd Lt. Herb Olshine, Major Mike Bavaro and 1st Lt. Keith Maxwell

The artillery order of Molly Pitcher recognizes individuals who have contributed in a significant way to the Field Artillery. It links these women in a sisterhood of voluntary contribution that perpetuates the symbolic heart and soul. Elayne, wife of an artillery man, was presented with a red and gold plaque, plus, a gold-tone neck chain with a medallion depicting Molly Pitcher to wear around her neck when attending any artillery affairs. Elayne says, "I didn't serve on the front lines, but shined a few shoes." I found Elayne with a sense of humor—what a joy! I am sure she did her share to earn such an honor.

"Molly Pitcher" was the nickname of the legendary figure of the American Revolutionary War. Her story is one of amazement. She carried pitchers of water to cool both the cannon and the fighting soldiers in her husband's battery. She assisted as an artillery gunner during the Battle of Monmouth in 1778 after her husband was wounded she took his place at the gun. She used a rammer—a rod that forces down the charge of a gun carriage. What a daring act! Word of her bravery reached General George Washington who personally issued her a warrant as a non-commissioned officer, and at the US Field Artillery Association in Fort Sill, Oklahoma known as "Sergeant Molly".

Mary Ludwig McCauley (Molly Pitcher), born in New Jersey, died in January 22, 1832, was buried along the Hudson River. Molly Pitcher was a legendary figure of the American Revolutionary War.

Jack has been active as well as President of his class at Princeton, University for years. His class celebrated its 70th Reunion in June 2007. One class member came back all the way from Switzerland, another from Florida, and another from Illinois. John is to be interviewed, photographed and all by a young fella from the New Jersey College. The young fella chose a very good source to interview, for John was in the Army before the Artillery went mobile. Then, I believe it was called Horse-Drawn Field Artillery before being sent to the 250th Field Artillery Battalion in Camp Maxey, Texas. He helped to form the 250th Field Artillery Battalion and served as commander of "C" Battery. He, also, served in the New Jersey Army National Guard.

Joe Festervan (top)

Joe's gun crew, (bottom) L–R: Tomball,
Wayne C. Ward, Cecil E. Aycock,
Joe Festervan and Frank L. Tovey

JOE FESTERVAN

B-BATTERY: ARTILLERY-GUNNER

I entered into the Army in December 1942. I was one of the first to be assigned to the 250th Field Artillery Battalion at Camp Maxey, Paris Texas.

A farm boy; the war wasn't hard for me like those that came from the city. I was use to work and responsibilities that was foreign to those young, inexperienced men still wet behind the ears.

As our battalion crossed France and Germany our basic training was very much appreciated. We had been placed under the command of two good field commanders' General Patton and Patch. The battalion spent a lot of time under Gen. LeClerc until Strasbourg where we were transferred to an American Tank Division.

There were times we would experience German tanks overrunning our US troops. The Air Force P-47 (Thunderbolt) would have to knock out the German tanks. The P-47 was a US single seat escort fighter and fighter-bomber. The P-47 would be the highest number of US planes built and operational from 1943-1955. It became the biggest and the heaviest as the war progressed. It was to be the last radial-engine fighter to serve in any number with the USAAF-US Army Air Force.

My tent partner, I became very close to. He was one of the older men drafted as the war progressed. He was in his thirties. His death was one of the hardest things I had to deal with. While we were in around the Bitche area Clarence McDonald was hit by shrapnel in the back of the head during a bombing. Clarence had been a heavy drinker and had said, "If I make it home I am going to make it up to my wife, a nurse, she would take and cover me up when I would be laying on the floor drunk." I never tried to make contact with his wife once I returned home. I now wish I would have to share with her his regrets and his desire to make it up to her. It may have been some comfort like my letters sent home were kept upbeat to reassure love ones.

In my section, Cecil Aycock was a short gun loader. Cecil would have the howitzer loaded before it got recoiled back. My job was to set the elevation level. I would calibrate the wheel that you turn up and down indicate values or position level aiming the stake on the bubble (like a level) to hit the target. After the howitzer is fired the barrel recoils from the explosion of the projectile. We were behind the infantry and if the shells fell short they would go on our Infantry. The foreword observers would radio to the commanding officer for our instructions on how we were to set our target. Cecil was fast and good.

When in bivouac there was always the worry of what was called "tree burst" where shells would burst in the trees and spread shrapnel all over—very dangerous!

Captured Germans prisoners would say, "I want to see that automatic artillery!" It could be so fast. The stock recoiled with a heavy spring that would take some of the shock off the kickback explosion and return to normal position.

The smell of death was overwhelming. The battalion reacted in a collectively state as much as we could and kept moving. There was much that our troops experienced—memories of burned comrades. It really would bother me to see our tanks on fire with 4-5 men. Once, a mortar shell fell in a direct hit in a foxhole leaving only shredded human flesh. You'd see fighter planes that had been shot down with its pilot's skeleton still in the seat of the plane—war is not pleasant!

While in Germany I went to a house looking for some food. There was a German Officer hiding in the barn. The people after asking about surrender told me about him being there. He gave no resistance and surrendered his German Lugar. He was fully armed and had a motorcycle with a sidecar.

After the war I was transferred with another outfit around the Danube River where we guarded a German Motor Pool. There were all kinds of vehicles that we centrally controlled with Austria civilians coming in. It was while I was here that I decided to take an Amphibious Jeep out on the river not knowing there was a hole underneath causing the motor to drown out about 100 yards from the shoreline. I thought—I went through the war without a scratch to now drown! The water being so swift took me down stream about a mile; by the grace of God—I made it back to shore! I don't to this day remember how?

While in Germany I would ride a motorcycle on Hitler's famous Autobahn just like a kid … there were some enjoyable moments! Being a gunner never gave one much free time.

After about three years I was on my way HOME by way of a small Liberty Ship. We passed through the Mediterranean, strait of Gibraltar to the Atlantic Ocean. The ship would jar you from the strong waves. We were about half way across the Atlantic when some of us decided to go up to the fan tail to sleep. Being down below the air was stale, musty—a fetid smell. Storms would build quickly with high waves. A large wave came up across the ship and lost some of the men. When they took roll call the next morning there were six men missing.

The trip took longer to get home, for the Atlantic was so rough that the propeller would come out of the water causing the captain to reduce the speed.

When the Battalion was at Strasbourg Cecil Aycock met and fell for a German girl named, Marie. He planned to go home to New Port, Virginia, for a visit with his family and then return to Marie. The Atlantic trip home was very rough and Cecil would get so sick and vomit. When asked if he was going back he replied, "I'll have to build a bridge before I'll go back!" There are so many stories, memories that each brought back. There was the wool underwear that caused an uncomfortable chaffing. They were meant for warmth, but instead left much discomfort for some of us men.

I was happy to serve my country. I returned home at the end of World War II in November 1945 with my mementos—a German Lugar and a gold watch. HOME, but not forgetting our fallen Brethren who walked the same steps, fought for the same reason, sought shelter from similar guns—but did not make it back. They were the heroes! Once home, I found success with much input of believing in being a doer' and proud for what we fought for—our country to be safe and free. What a journey for our 250th Field Artillery Battalion!

In 2006 I wrote Joe's Autobiography: Success in Believing–an Inspiring Story of Joe Festervan. I didn't know much about Joe until I wrote his story. Joe, through hard work and determination, has done well for himself. In my research for Joe's book, I found Joe to be a giver. A person that *quietly* does things for those in need. He is a very upfront type person, but a little reserved.

Milton Broussard: 20–21 years old

Milton J. Broussard

HEADQUARTERS' BATTERY

*M*ilton always had a storehouse of stories that he would share with everyone. He would spend hours pouring over his memories of war stories. Milton probably is reliving the happy memories of the many reunions and those whose life he touched so long ago. The reunions have become a centerpiece of perhaps some of Milton's happiest times. Two years ago, he brought a plastic bag of Mardi Gras beads from the New Orleans' festivities for our two granddaughters. It was amazing that he recalled Carl and I had two granddaughters. His reaching out—remembering was a wonderful gesture.

Goldie, Milton's wife, sent a copy of a 1982 reunion report. In it there was a story about after the war while the 250th Battalion was assigned to a rest camp close to Salzburg, called Camp Mattsee. In the Stars and Stripe newsletter there was an article published about Hungarian treasure found in Rosenleim, Germany, on July 1, 1945. In a cache there was Royal Hungarian treasure valued at 75,000,000 dollars, including the Holy Hand of St. Stephen was discovered at Mattsee, 13 miles northeast of Salzburg. The cache was later turned back over to the Hungarian Government. Hungarian's war debt to the United States had held up the jewels that had been recovered from a church at Mattsee.

The 250th Battalion served with great pride through Normandy, Northern

France, Alsace-Ardennes, Rhineland and Central Europe Campaigns were a major contribution to Allied victory. Milton served with the 250th Headquarters' Battery. A strong, believer in God; found prayer helped him to get though the ordeals he faced in war time. He carried his rosary most of the time. The belief in miracles was a direct support for Milton.

Milton served as the 250th Field Artillery Battalion's Headquarters' Battery Coordinator for the 250th reunions. His wife, Goldie, a former school teacher, was one of the first to welcome Carl and me at our first reunion. Goldie has been a very active participant; assisting Rosie Yuratich at the reunions. Rosie is the 250th Battalion's secretary. Milton and Goldie played a major role with the annual reunions over the years. Milton served as the reunion's Headquarters Battery Coordinator for several years.

There are many war stories; Milton has a great compulsion to relate the stories of heroism in the forests of France and Germany. He loves the American Dream—freedom and liberty. I am not sure what Milton's job was with headquarters, but I can rest you assured—you knew he was there! He talked a lot about General LeClerc. In 1979, a group from the 250th Battalion made a *special* trip to Europe for the 35th Anniversary of D-Day. They attended celebrations at both Omaha and Utah Beaches, visited the Falaise Gap area, and then on to Paris where a banquet was held in the 250th Battalion's honor by the 2nd French Armored Division. The group enjoyed visiting familiar sights of the battalion's World War II route. The highlight at Strasbourg was the presence of General LeClerc's widow. LeClerc was quite an interesting general with a strong will of determination. Our Allied showed much determination, too. Those that were fortunate to return came home to never forget. While on foreign soil, like Milton, many turned to their faith for reassurance of His presence.

L-R: Dick Adair & Jeff F. Adair (top)

Dick Adair: Supplies (bottom left)

International Boundary Block (bottom right)
Germany & Austria 500 yards

DICK ADAIR

SERVICE BATTERY: RATION AND SUPPLIES

JEFF ADAIR

SERVICE BATTERY: CAPTAIN HIGH'S RADIO OPERATOR

*W*e were brothers serving together as we always had. Before our enlisting we worked at Safe-Way Grocery. Dick worked in the meat department and I worked in produce.

The enlistment was being closed, but there was the draft law, "Selective Act Service" in force. There were twelve of us from our county that enlisted together. Dick was the first to be sworn in and I was the last on December 9, 1943. Dick's serial number was 12 digits smaller than mine. For two days we messed in and around Headquarters in Oklahoma City. From Oklahoma City on December 11th, we were sent to Fort Sills, Oklahoma. At the induction center, they kept Dick as typist, for they didn't have anyone to type. He had gone two years to Oklahoma University. There were plans to send me to Camp Robinson, Arkansas, but Dick and I went to the Chaplin. He stopped my being transferred. While Dick typed, I messed around for two months. Fort Sills was an artillery training center.

I was 18 and Dick was 20 when we enlisted. After two months we were sent to Camp Maxey, Paris, Texas on December 20th, 1943 to the 250th Field Artillery Battalion. Dick was assigned to Ration Supply and I was assigned to Headquarters as machine gunner where I operated a 50 caliber machine gun. It had been agreed that Dick and I would be kept together. I was reassigned six weeks later to Service Battery as Captain High's radio operator. Captain High was Service Battery Commander. I would receive orders from Headquarters to Captain High. Dick was assigned to Rations Supply from his experience being a meat cutter. Dick worked with Fred Bush and Howard Clanton. Clanton was the supply truck driver. They supplied Headquarters, A, B, C, Batteries and Service Battery. They went every morning to get supplies and rations. They were kept on the move without much R & R.

The battalion was being prepared for overseas duties. We left on a two-day train ride from Camp Maxey, Paris, Texas for New York where we were sent to Camp Shanks. We left the New York Harbor on the Dominion Monarch. The Atlantic was so rough; it made you a little queasy. There was nothing to do but lay around on your so-called-bed. We landed in Liverpool, England and then to Camp Atherstone and various other places for more training. We guarded German prisoners taken during the invasion of Normandy before we left Southampton for France. We arrived at Utah Beach on July 21, 1944. The Normandy Beach had been chosen for D-Day invasion because of its weaker defense.

Everyone but the Ration Supply men and the medics had to take turns on KP and night watch detail. We set up our 50 caliber machine gun outpost. We had four hour watch—not leaving our post.

I was there when Charley Johnson of Service Battery was injured. There was a plane that went over and Charlie went running for protection at a rock fence when he was hit. We didn't take him serious when he said that he had been hit by anti-aircraft shell. Charley was always scared—nervous! He had a serious injury.

When we got ready to come home, Dick had 5 more points than I had. I had 80 and Dick had 85, for he was married and had earned a Bronze Star. Dick refused to leave until I got my points.

We were sent to Plzeň, Czechoslovakia where we shipped out on December 12, 1945. As we boarded the Liberty ship there was a welder welding a crack from the inside. We said, "We hoped you do a good job! We heard there were some Liberty ships that had broken apart out on the sea." The welder must have done a good job; the sea was so rough that the ship's bow went up and back down to hit another wave. There were colored soldiers down below the bow. They were so scared they came up out from the bow. It was said—they had a color scared white!

We were supposed to land on the December 20th in New York, City. We got into a storm and landed in Boston on Christmas Day. From Boston it was back to New York and Camp Shanks where our embarkation was from when we went to Europe crossing the Atlantic, in a large convoy on February 11, 1944.

From Camp Shanks we went by train to Camp Fannin near Tyler, Texas on December 31st. There was an Army Captain from Dallas that said he would take five of us at $30. each to Dallas. We arrived in Dallas, Texas at 6:00 p.m. on January 1, 1946 to catch a train. Dick left by bus for Oklahoma City to meet his wife, Mildred. I and another fella from Wichita, Kansas went to the train station. It was a big train station, we had to go into a gate and down a long hallway to the gate track wanted—it was gate 8 or 10. When we got to the gate an older fella ask where we were going and we told him Oklahoma, City. He said, "This is not the right gate, you have to go back and see where you are to go." We walked all the way back only to be told at the same gate where we had been that it was time for the train. We got back to the gate just as the train was pulling away. Boy! I could have hit the guy, but I wouldn't.

I went to a travel agency. It was New Years Eve and had to set around waiting for a car. I was getting impatient. There were two ladies that owned the agency; I told them I would give them one hundred dollars to take me to the bus station at Oklahoma, City. They drove me there but I missed the bus; it was about 4:00 in the morning. The two ladies told me if I would give them $60 dollars they'd take me to 705 N. 12th Street Enid, OK. We arrived at 6:00 a.m. on January 1,

1945. I said thank you, but they just sat there. I told them they could go on for it was where I lived, but they said, "We want to see your mother's reaction when she sees you." Upon opening the door my Mother gave me a hug. The ladies waved and drove away.

Good friend and brother, Richard Adair, passed away in August of 1993. Dick and Jeff Adair were two brothers that served together … an adhering bond that one can admire. I found it was hard for Jeff to talk—I didn't push him. Dick's wife, Mildred, shared with me that after Dick returned home he said, "That after the war was announced over some of them were down in this valley with men above them celebrating big time. It was dangerous; someone could easy have gotten hurt."

Walter Yuratich (top)

*Walter and his gun crew, (bottom) and some
"C" Battery men. Walter's head is against
the Howitzer (photo center)*

WALTER YURATICH

ARTILLERY C-BATTERY: HOWITZER GUNNER

A Country Boy Goes to War….It all started in late November 1942 as I returned home from work in late afternoon. My mom said, "You have an important letter from the White House in Washington, D.C." I had just turned 21 years of age in October. The letter was very interesting—it started off with "Greetings from the president of the United States" and went on telling me that I would soon be a member of the United States Military. They would feed me, clothe me, and pay me $50 a day. What a change from my little salary I was getting from my job I had. The only thing was that the $50-a-day was to be paid only once a month! After paying my mother's allotment, I received only $17 that I could call my own.

I was sworn in on December 17, 1942, in New Orleans with about 80 other men. The officer in charge—a very generous man gave some of us the choice of going to camp now or we could return home for 7 days. I selected home for seven more days that meant I was to report back on Christmas day. Well, someone had a heart as big as a pea and let us report back on December 26th.

I left home on December 26th after a day of celebrating with my family: 4:30 a.m. came very early. Saying goodbye was very hard on my mother, two sisters and brother, but Uncle Sam said be happy and get on the bus—it will take you to Camp Beauregard, LA. That's where I was issued a uniform that didn't fit, shoes that were two sizes too large, shirts that the neck buttoned down to my waist. The blouse as the army called it was fine. To me, it was a coat! They issued me two pair of winter pants and two khakis and shirts to match. After sending all civilian clothes home, I was too hot to trot. I'm in the army now and can't do a dang thing about it!

We were issued leggings that no one knew what to do with, a service belt, canteen cup, mess kit, knife and fork and spoon—all aluminum. First day at breakfast had powdered eggs and something that looked like ham and hot coffee. The cup was so hot that 'til today I have *no* taste for hot coffee—my lips still burn!

On December 28th we all boarded the train for parts unknown, no one tells you anything. On the morning of December 29th the train pulled into a siding at Camp Maxey; didn't know if it was California, New York or Tim-buck-too. We were herded into trucks and taken to our new home away from home. Before bedtime we went to a place called the mess hall. We were served sauerkraut and hot dogs. That's why they say you never forget your first day at camp.

Next morning some goofy guy comes through the building before daylight blowing a whistle and yelling "everyone out of bed and fall out." Whatever fallout meant we all went outside, it was at that time we were told that we were near Paris, Texas. Basic training began that day. By the way—that "goofy guy" was our 1st Sgt. Wentz. After breakfast a sergeant came into the barracks and started showing us how to make a bed. Then all went out to the drill field. That's where you are told you have two feet—left and right!

We went through basic training with flying colors, except that Haslet could never learn how to march. He was always out of step. The Sergeant would yell, "Haslet, changed step." Poor Haslet, three more steps again out of step. Finally the Sergeant would yell, "Everybody but Haslet change step." Well, that didn't work so eventually poor Haslet was discharged and sent home.

Next in line were the Louisiana maneuvers. That's where I was introduced to the Razorback hogs (thin bodied long-legged feral), ticks, chiggers, and the first time seeing an armadillo. One crawled in my tent one night and scared me half to death; funny for some—but not yours truly! Their body and head are encased in an armor of small bony plates.

We returned to Camp Maxey for last minute training, then after a few weeks we were ready for a long train ride to New York. We saw some real tall buildings and a few night clubs. We had much fun but knew it would soon end. On the third night we boarded buses for a short trip to the waterfront where we boarded an English ship (Dominion Monarch). I awoke the next morning to the rolling Atlantic Ocean and was sick as a dog from that day 'til the ship docked in Liverpool, England. My home then was old WWI barracks in Atherstone, England. The battalion received further training while waiting orders to cross the English Channel. We shipped out on July 18, 1944, for the shores of Normandy, France. My first night on shore was a sensation that I will never forget. The German planes were strafing the many ships moored on the Channel, as well as the shoreline where I had dug a foxhole deep enough to hold most of the U.S. Army. I said more prayers that first night on shore than I had said before or since. The good lord was good to me because here I am writing these few things that I remember. Trying to remember things that happened 60 years ago is taxing my brain to its fullest. After a day or so, the battalion was again at full strength and we began our march across France. We went through many villages, towns, and cities. On our way we were assigned to the French 2nd Armored Division—the best fighting men under the leadership of General LeClerc, a French General who formed a division of its own from men who had fought in North Africa.

The 250th Battalion was attached to three armies: 1st, 3rd, and 7th. Three army corps: V, VI, XV, many divisions: 14 in all, while fighting through France and into Germany, our long miserable ride through the Vosges Mountains into the city of Strasbourg. It was there that my gun, the 1st Section 105 Howitzer fired the first shell into Germany. That was such an honor for me and the men of the 1st Section: Chitman, Ramos, Beuche, Pulse, Sisk and myself. From the beginning of my three years in the army I was blessed to have what I think were the two best commanding officers in the 250th. First was Capt. Eberhardt, then later, Capt. Herbert Glazer.

Capt. Eberhardt was the first in promoting me to from PFC to Corporal. I was again the first man promoted in the 250th. Later on in Salzburg, Capt. Glazer promoted me to a Sergeant. I still keep in touch with two of the finest men that I have ever met. These two men that I will never forget took me through World War II and sent me home in one piece to my family—Thank God! The war is something I very seldom talk about. My son is now a doctor often asks me about my war years. I don't say much. He's very interested about hearing about the war that his father was in. One time he asked me if I had killed many Germans. All I could tell him was that I fired the shells, where they landed I don't know. The men up front are the only ones that knew. World War II is an experience that the men *who* returned will *never* forget! We will let history do our talking.

I went to our local high school for a program our VFW Post was involved in. I was ashamed to report to my post the lack of interest that the high school students had about the war: who we were fighting, where is Japan and Germany? The high schools and colleges had better get busy teaching these kids about things they should know, or all of our years will be forgotten in a short time! World War II as Archie Bunker said, "The "BIG ONE" will vanish from our school books.

I gave three years of my life for our country. I'm proud of what I was able to do. PLEASE don't let all our efforts be forgotten. I received many citations and served with and for some of the greatest men of our era: Generals Eisenhower, Patton, Bradley, Patch, Haislip and LeClerc. Let's not forget the head men—Presidents Roosevelt and Truman.

The above story is a beginning, but not the end of Walter's story. Walter and wife, Rosie, have been two of the major forces of the 250th Reunions. I love and respect them both! I would have never known what a wonderful group the 250th is *if not* for Walter Yuratich and our VFW magazine seven years ago.

In 2006 Walter sent me sixteen *personally* hand written pages of his life, which I used to write "Louisiana Boy—From World War II to Katrina". It was a hard story to write, for there was so much pain and hardship to write about. They lost everything during Katrina. Walter and Rosy relocated to Littleton, Colorado near their daughter, Sharon and son-in-law, Al Johnson. Walter found he had cancer in 2007. Walter is giving it a good fight.

Wallace A. Reid

WALLACE A. REID

B-BATTERY: ARTILLERY-GUNNER

*I*n the '30s Germany had all Europe scared that war was approaching. My father had served in WWI and was sure that the United States would be involved. I wanted to enlist, but mother and father didn't want me to until I had finished high school. I kept bugging them until they let me enlist in December of 40 although I was only seventeen years old. The army boarded me in a hotel in Jackson, Mississippi, and provided me a meal ticket at a café. I stayed there two weeks until more men enlisted. The officer in charge entrusted me with the paper work on sixteen people of which I was in charge. I was the youngest in the group and felt honored to be trusted.

The next day we left Jackson by train and traveled to Ft. Jackson, S.C. We arrived two days later after midnight and were picked up by an open truck in Columbia, S.C., and transported to Ft. Jackson. The C.Q. threw each of us a blanket and told us where to bunk. He said there was a stove and some coal to use for heat. We never could get the funnel stove started in order to heat the tent in which we were to sleep. We wrapped up in the blanket and lay on an army cot but didn't get any sleep. The Mess Sergeant came by about 4:00 a.m. and assigned me to K.P. and about 8:00 a.m. I was running a fever. I told the sergeant I was sick, so he sent me on sick call. They put me in the hospital where I stayed two weeks.

When I recovered I reported to my battalion which was Hq Btry 1st Bat. 83 Reg. The first Sgt. told a corporal to take me down and show me where to bunk; after he got me settled he left. I went back to the orderly room and surprisingly saw that corporal again. I received my bedding and returned to the barrack and lo and behold, there was that same corporal again. I said, "Man, you're the fastest person I have ever seen!" Later, I learned he was J. E. Morris and had identical twin, C.E. Morris. It took me about a year before I could tell them apart.

When I began basic training at Ft. Jackson, my drill sergeant was Sgt. Wintz, and drill officer was Lt. Bavaro. As soon as we finished basic training, First Sgt. Lucas called me in and said, "Reid, I've been watching you." I thought, man, I'm in trouble now. However, he asked, "How would you like to be the guidon carrier?" I told him I would, but my dad told me never to volunteer for anything. He asked, "What does he know about the Army?" I told him my dad was in the Marines, Infantry, and Coast Artillery, and during WWI he served in the Army Air Forces during his time in service. He replied, "I understand, but this is a good job and it calls for a rank of corporal." I gladly accepted the job and made corporal after four months in the service. This job increased my pay from twenty-one dollars to thirty-six dollars a month. This was horse drawn artillery regiment, so we had to learn to ride. As the guidon carrier, I also had to carry messages from our battery headquarter to Regimental Headquarters.

A frightening incident occurred while we were bivouacked out in the boondocks. I had to deliver a message to Regimental Headquarters. My horse got spooked by a piece of paper, and I lost control of him. He was running full speed as I approached Regimental Headquarters and headed for a group of high ranking officers talking around a table. They scattered like a bunch of quail as the horse ran right through the table and chairs and threw me over his head right into some plum bushes; luckily, I didn't break any bones but was skinned up badly. I was chewed out pretty good, but I didn't get busted. They took pity on me because I was real young and scared.

First Sgt. Lucas, whom I previously mentioned, was a professional boxer and fought for the light weight championship, but he didn't win. He had a gym set up in an empty building. Every time a bunch of recruits arrived he looked them over;

he wanted to find someone to make a good boxer. One day he said, "Reid, I want you to come out for boxing; you might make my boxing team." I replied' "Sgt. Lucas, I've never boxed in my life." He said, "I just want you to try out." Well, I started working out with the rest of the team. During my boxing career I had a real good record; I just lost one fight, of course, that was my first fight and my last.

A few weeks later we heard a rumor that we were going to Ft. Sill, Oklahoma. We were all excited thinking maybe we would see some of those pretty Indian girls. In June, we loaded on trains and headed for Ft. Sill, OK. We loaded guns, horses, and all of our equipment. The trip took nearly a week because we stopped each night and unloaded the horses so they could be exercised. We always stopped near some small town, so we could be pulled off on a railroad siding to unload. We stopped in towns in Tennessee, Arkansas, and Oklahoma before arriving at Ft. Sill. I remember it was the first of June, and it rained nearly every day; the climate sure changed since then. Also, while on the train we saw a farmer plowing on Sunday. We were stunned because we had never seen anyone work on Sunday. After we were settled, we received some new horses from Ft. El Reno that had only been broken bareback. I was put on remount detail to help break them to saddle. I was thrown nearly everyday.

On the 4th of July a couple of my friends and I traveled to Craterville Park for a big annual celebration. While there I met my wife's sister and later visited her family in Grandfield, where I met my future wife Margie and fell in love.

In September, 1941, we became motorized and phased out our horses. I was so proud we didn't have to take care of horses anymore. I remember Dec. 7, 1941, when Japan bombed us. I was in a picture show in downtown Lawton, OK, and they stopped the movie and told all servicemen to report to base. It was a scary time because we thought we would be shipped right out over to fight Japan, which didn't happen. However, soon after Pearl Harbor I applied for radio school which I completed the next year, 1942.

In September, 1942, I cadred out from Ft. Sill, OK, to Camp Maxey, Texas, to help form a new Artillery Battalion which was the 250th. We started receiving our men in November, December, and January. These men were the cream of the crop; they were the easiest to train. Consequently, we had the best reputation in the entire European theater and every division wanted our artillery support. After we completed training them, we went to Louisiana maneuvers in the summer of 1943.

In December we received orders to report to Camp Shanks, N.J. All of our girlfriends and wives wanted to come see us off, but we were restricted to base and couldn't leave to meet them. I gave a picture of Margie to the wife of one of the men, "Red" Lashley, and asked her to meet Margie at the bus station and bring her out to Camp Maxey. She located Margie and brought her to meet me at the M.P. gate where our train was already loaded for departure.

When we arrived at Camp Shanks, New Jersey, the temperature was below 0 degrees. We were tested there for overseas duty, and I heard we passed the highest Field Artillery score that had ever been recorded. The 18th FABn which was also tested failed the test and had to return to California for more training, and later were sent to the South Pacific instead of Europe.

On February 11, 1944, we loaded on the Dominion Monarch, a British ship, which was part of a one-hundred nine ship convoy. It was of the largest convoy to cross the Atlantic Ocean during the war. The crossing took us twelve days, and we landed in Liverpool, England, on February 23, 1944. We were transported by small trains to Atherstone. We were stationed at Camp Marevale, a small British camp, with only our battalion and a Quarter Master Company that did laundry. In June we left Atherstone and convoyed to Oldham, which is near Manchester, England, where we did guard duty for German prisoners of war.

After a few weeks we loaded up and moved to Southampton and boarded a ship for France. We were on the U.S.S. Herkimer and conveyed to Utah Beach on the coast of Normandy, France. I failed to mention that General Patton chose us as part of the 3rd Army.

A funny thing happened while we were bivouacked in an apple orchard. We received a gas alarm and John L. Wann left his gas mask in an apple tree and couldn't get it down, so he just unzipped it and put it over his face. He looked like he was hitched like a horse. We were in hedgerow country and it was very hard to advance against the Germans, but we were able to move slowly. Some of the towns we went through were just rubble, like St. Lo and LeMan; we would go into position, fire, then move into a new position, fire, and move again. We were transferred from one division to another, but the one I liked the best was the French 2nd Armored Division, which we were attached to more often than any of the other divisions. When the Battle of Falaise was over, several of us went into the impact area looking for souvenirs. I found a French Renault; it was a black four door convertible with red leather upholstery. The car wouldn't start, but someone thought it might be out of gas. A while later someone came by with some gas; we got it started and went back to the battery. We painted big white stars on each side to be safe from aircraft. First Sgt. Anderson and I took it for our personal car, but Quarter Master Corp made us turn it in.

While at the Falasie Gap, Cpl. Draper and I found some bee hives at an abandoned chateau, he assured me that he knew all about robbing bee hives, so we found some large containers from our kitchen truck and filled them. We decided we would get some more containers and fill them and have the cooks make pancakes for everyone. When we returned to the hives, the bees were real mad and nearly stung us to death, so we didn't get any more honey. However, we did have pancakes with the honey we had already collected.

One day we were in position and had just gotten paid, a few of us were having a poker game when we heard an aircraft overhead; we thought the planes were ours so we didn't pay any attention until someone looked up and said they were German planes. We all made a run for some trees so we could get out of the line of fire, but Marshall Roy, our machine gunner, made a run for his gun that was set up in a fox hole and started shooting at the planes. When they came back over, he hit one of the planes, and it crashed. He received credit for the hit because an anti Air Craft unit was up the road and told us that Marshall Roy had shot down one of the planes.

One night we had a strange thing happen; some Germans were trying to get back to their unit and stumbled into our unit. We had quite a fire fight. The next morning, Byrd Lewis and Canter were out walking along some manure when they saw a hand sticking out of a pile of manure. They pulled the German soldier out and kicked out six more soldiers. One of the soldiers was an officer, and he had a German Lugar that I took from him. We were not sure we had accounted for all of them so we made a sweep through a wooded area about a mile by one-half mile wide. We didn't find any more Germans; but we found a large hog. Consequently, someone killed him for the kitchen. I don't remember if we ate him or not. Major Bavaro arrived about that time; he noticed the German Lugar and told me he wanted the gun. I said, "I want it, too." He replied, "Well, you'll have another chance to get one and I won't," so I let him have it. However, I never had the opportunity to get another Lugar.

As we were moving eastward toward Germany, we maneuvered into a firing position in a field late in the evening. Since it was misting rain, we put up a tarp between some trees to get under as we pulled guard duty. I happened to be Sgt. of guard that night. I set up with the first shift, and we talked until time to change guards. Habernigg, our mail clerk, had come down from headquarters and didn't have anyone to pitch a pup tent with, so I told him to sleep in the radio equipment truck, which he did because it had a cover over it. I warned to be careful about getting up without letting the guards know. I had barely crawled in my tent when I heard a halt three times and then firing. The guard shouted, "Germans are all around me." I jumped up and when I reached the guard I asked him, "Did you shoot Habernigg?" He said, "No, I didn't. He's in the truck." I crawled over to the truck and discovered he wasn't there. I knew then that Habernigg had been shot, but I crawled out to where he was gurgling and felt of his dog tags. The Germans wore leather ones and ours were metal. We called headquarters and they sent the doctor, and I remember seeing the jeep appearing with someone in front guiding him with a flashlight. I'm not positive, but he was probably our first casualty in B-Battery.

As we moved eastward, we stopped about 10 miles out of Luneville. Jack Draper, Hoffmand, and I started to build a half dugout, logs up so high, and then our pup tent was on top. While there we found some German grenades and decided we could kill some fish in a little stream that ran by our position, which we did. I would go in the water for a while, and then we would trade off. We retrieved quite a few fish and our cook fixed them for us. The little fishing episode cost me because I came down with pneumonia and the doctor wanted to send me back to the rear to a hospital, but I begged him to let me stay. I knew if

I went back I would never get to return to my unit, so he kept treating me there because we stayed quite awhile, maybe two weeks.

The Germans had dug a trench on top of a ridge about a mile long overlooking Baccarat. We pushed them off and took over and used it for observation. As we were walking one day, we saw these two young GI'S in a slit trench talking and laughing. When we went down later that evening we stopped by to talk to them; however, both were dead because an artillery shell had landed in the hole with them.

The next day there were some tanks below the ridge firing over us toward the Germans, and we were watching; a GI would run to his foxhole when a German round was coming in, then he would stick his foot or hand up in the air. While we were observing, he didn't quite make it to the foxhole. I suppose he was trying for a trip home; he made the trip all right but not alive.

While we were in the Luneville area, Sgt. Grubbs, Sgt. Honey, Sgt. Alridge, and I decided to get permission to drive to Rhemes, France. Sgt. Alridge had a brother that was stationed there with the Air Force; Capt. Lewis said it was okay. We started out early the next morning; there was a lot of fog and it was hard to see; suddenly, we saw this big buck deer standing beside the road; we thought we would kill him and take him back to the battery. Therefore, we all took a shot but not a one of us hit him; we were used to shooting 105's not thirty caliber rifles.

After leaving the Baccarat area, we started toward Strasbourg; we were driving in the dark. On the way my truck driver was tired so I volunteered to drive him. Of course we drove in black out, as we were traveling through a small village. I ran into a shell hole, and we had to be pulled out. It didn't do any damage because I was driving so slowly. I can remember the kitchen trucks feeding us turkey and dressing for Thanksgiving dinner on the road to Strasbourg.

Lt. Triumpho, Guy Bolden, and I traveled with the French Liaison team to Strasbourg and arrived after dark. Some F.F.I. men hid us in a warehouse which we thought was empty, and all night we could smell whisky, so the next morning, Bolden and I went upstairs where we were surprised to find it full of cognac. We grabbed a couple of gallons and took them back to the Battery. We gave the gun crew most of it; it was really cold and they needed it.

After we took over Strasbourg, some of us were staying in a pump station, and we could look across the river into Germany. The Germans had not blown the bridge, so we were firing on the German's side to keep them from blowing it up. The 250th Field Artillery Battalion was given credit and recognized for firing the first rounds across the Rhine River on German soil. Other troops came into Strasbourg, and we left moving south because there was supposed to be a large German force; however, we couldn't find them, so we headed back north. A friend of mine, Bill Humphrey that lives here in Grandfield, OK, was taken prisoner at Strasbourg after we left the area. He was a prisoner until the war ended.

Lt. Triumpho, Guy Bolden, and I had been to our F.O. position all day on December 11, 1944. We arrived back at our gun position about dark. All night we received incoming artillery rounds, which kept us jumping from pup tent to foxhole. About daylight I walked to our kitchen truck for some coffee. After receiving the coffee, I returned to see if anyone had been hurt that night. Some of the men had built a small fire and were standing around waiting for breakfast. About the time I arrived, an artillery round came in hitting a tree about 15 to 20 feet from us cutting the tree off about three feet high. Of the six men there, four of us were hit; I didn't know I was injured until I got up from the ground to go to the switchboard to call for the medics. Soon Captain Lewis and someone, maybe a medic, brought a weapon carrier, driven by Elvin Williams. They loaded us up, and as we were pulling away someone shouted to stop. They needed my shoepacs' because everyone didn't have a pair. My feet nearly froze on the way to the field hospital, which was several miles behind the lines.

From the field hospital, I was taken to a station hospital, which was a larger facility, where my surgery was performed. While I was there, a German plane bombed us at night. He was flying too low and crashed and burned. A few days after Christmas of 1944 I was moved to a small air strip to be flown to Paris, France, but the fog was so bad that the pilot couldn't land the plane. A few days later we were loaded on a train, just cattle cars, no heat. We nearly froze. In January, we were loaded a C47 plane to be sent to Bristol, English, to a larger hospital. Before take off the pilot came by and talked to us. While at the hospital, I saw Joe Hammond who was wounded when I was. I think he went back to the 250th.

After I was discharge from Legarde General Hospital in New Orleans, LA, Margie and I were married on March 29, 1945, at the First Baptist church in Crystal Springs, Mississippi. We moved to Grandfield, Ok, in June 1945. One day I was walking down the sidewalk in town when I saw a man that looked real familiar; after talking to him, both of us realized he was the pilot who flew us to England. He had flown his brother Lewis Purcell from a P.O.W. camp after the war. His name was Jack Purcell and Grandfield was his hometown and now my adopted town.

Later, I enrolled at Oklahoma University, but found out Margie was expecting, and the government didn't pay enough on the G.I. Bill. So I took a job at the Bell Oil and Gas Refinery, as a lab tech. I checked oils and gases before they were shipped. In 1960, I went to work for the army in the guided missile department and retired after twenty-six and one-half years.

We had one son, Wallace Austin Reid, Jr. and three daughters. Our son Wallace was in the army during the Vietnam War and served as a captain. After active duty, he attended law school and received his Juris Doctorate. Wallace Jr., was killed in California in 1981. Our three daughters, Johnnie, Kathy, and Gwen are currently active teachers. We have eight grandchildren and nine great grandchildren. All of our grandchildren have or are working toward their degrees as follows: Brigette Tisdale, Doctorate in Pharmacy; Michael Baughman, BS in Secondary Education/Sports Medicine; James Reid, Marketing Executive and is completing his BA degree; Monica Wilke, Juris Doctorate; Jon Miller, Physical Therapist; Brain Reid Stoddard, is completing his BS in Secondary Education; Henry Reid, Masters of Computer Science Engineering; and Travis Baughman is in the final year of completing his Doctorate of Pharmacy.

Wallace & wife, Margie (top)

Wallace Reid was wounded in action in France on December 11, 1943, and was discharged from hospital in June 1945 and sent home (bottom)

Carl E. Gwin: Salzburg, Austria—1945

CARL E. GWIN

HEADQUARTERS: SERVICE BATTERY-MEDIC

*A*merica was challenged and answered the challenge when World War II hit full stride. It was a time in history that would remain graphic for us soldiers. Many of us came home as we went in—quietly, with no fan fare! More than anything, we each wanted to get back home, but never to forget our fallen comrades.

I never received a card saying: "Greetings, you have been selected by your draft board to serve in the Army." I was going to Purdue University and was in ROTC when I chose to enlist; I could have gotten a farm deferment as many did. My brother had been drafted in 1941 and was serving as a hospital medic in the Pacific Theater. I didn't want to be back here in college while he was over amongst the fighting. I had trouble getting the army to accept me due to a heart murmur. After I wrote asking for combat duty; they obliged me. They evidently got tired of my bothering them and I entered the Army on May 13, 1943.

I soon learned just how the army does things. There were bedrolls, duffle bags, and pup tents, changing clothes, inspection drills, long hikes, hurried meals, sleepless nights all the making of a good soldier; where boys became men.

I was classified as a Surgical Technician at Camp Robinson in Little Rock, Arkansas, where I did my basic training with Co. "C" 104th Medic Training Battalion. From Camp Robinson I was sent to Brownsville Depot to Camp

Maxey, Paris, Texas replacement center. There I served with Headquarters' Medical Corp. I was one of 12 medics assigned to the 250th Battalion. I was assigned with B-Battery to later be transferred to Service Battery where I spent the rest of my time until reassigned after V-E Day.

If the quota hadn't been filled I would have been sent to OCS—Officers Candidate School. I declined the "ASTP" Army Specialized Training Program. It was a college program, which is why I declined to participate. I didn't want to be restricted.

From Camp Maxey we were put on the train not knowing if ear-marked east for Europe or west for Japan. Our arrival at Camp Shanks, New York, was our stop off for shipment for overseas—bound for Europe.

On February 11, 1944 on the Dominion Monarch, we left the New York Port in a conglomeration; a large convoy escorted by air-craft carriers and naval vessels crossing the North Atlantic. We arrived in Liverpool, England on February 23, 1944—two days before my 20th birthday. Liverpool looked pretty good, for we were back on land. We had more training and assigned guard detail of German prisoners taken on June 6, 1944 D-Day in Europe.

I treated 3 German prisoners that had tried to escape, and the fourth was killed. I gave each a morphine shot to ease their pain. Barney Howard and I talked on the phone before the 2004 reunion. Jokingly, Barney said, "Hey, Doc, I need a shot!" He went on to say he wanted the two of us to go off to a corner and have some tea together for he said, "I want to ask you a question." The question was something my wife, Ruby, asks me, too—was it necessary for Crutchfield to kill the one German prisoner that was trying to escape? I answered the best I could, I told Barney—"If the circumstance were different he would have killed us!" Perhaps it was an accident on Crutchfield's part. I don't want to believe he shot to kill. As I look back, it was the best answer I could give Barney. I can't be the judge on that day so long ago.

Barney, as Ruby had a right to ask—was it necessary? We were young men making decisions that had to be made—one can only hope it was the right one! When assigned a mission you follow through the best one can. War is not pleasant, but ugly; everything should be done to avoid one. The simple truth is—soldiers had to kill or be killed!

The prisoners were treated well while in our hands. I was the one that cared for those placed with Service Battery that called for medical attention; I gave them good care. They ate the food we ate. It was more than what can be said about our captured soldiers, they were brutally mistreated.

We left entering the English Channel from Southampton on the U.S.S. Herkimer and arrived on the Normandy coast. The English Channel was too rough making it unsafe to disembark. After 4-5 days on ship, we disembarked by rope over the ship's side. A large number of other ships were waiting to unload. On the front of the ships there were blimps (nonrigid airship) anchored with a cable on a hook to prevent German airplanes from coming in and strafing the ships.

The 250th Field Artillery Battalion served under General Haislip and assigned with two of the best field commanders' General Patton and General Patch. General Patton had chosen the 250th Field Artillery Battalion in January of 1944 from their jacket training. The 250th at different times were assigned to General LeClerc for he liked the 250th Field Artillery support.

General LeClerc was actually a "count", and took the LeClerc name to protect family. He commanded the Second French Armored Division. General LeClerc was on a mission. He had been captured by the Boches twice and escaped both times. The liberation of Strasbourg was important for the French. The Germans had taken over all Alsace for many years and had possession of Strasbourg. The Germans had imposed the German language on all Alsace.

Falaise Gap was one area that stands out for me. There was carnage lying everywhere in charred ruins. It was haunting! The gap was a narrow strip of land through foreign-held territory, a death trap situation that was very dangerous. It almost immobilized one with terror. When the fighting got so intensified, some of our young soldiers felt they wouldn't make it back home.

We were a lucky bunch; our being detained on the U.S.S. Herkimer ship after we arrived on the coast of Normandy. It would be here the battalion got their first taste of war to move on to follow behind the ferocious fighting through St. Lô. The St. Lô "Cobra Operation" area the First Army suffered large casualties, 90% were infantrymen. Meanwhile, we were under the capable command of

General Countney Hodge's First Army until General Patton's arrival. We would never have gotten through St. Lô without casualties; tons of explosives had been used leaving nothing but destruction. St. Lô was the breakthrough for the Normandy battle. It was where we encountered hedgerows that the Germans could conceal their weapons and tanks behind. It was very dangerous and the Allied paid for every foot taken with a casualty. The origin of the Normandy hedgerows dates back to Roman times.

General Patton arrived on July 31, 1944, from Northern England where he had been as decoy preparing his Third Army for the invasion. Patton's coming in from the west surprised the Germans for they were expecting him to come in from the east. Once Patton got to Normandy he sprung loose the Third Army moving with his usual sudden speed. We encountered fog, supply and gas shortages. Patton was fervent to keep pushing on. The longest we ever had to wait for gas supply was outside of Paris. We waited there for a week.

The day before Thanksgiving, after heavy fighting since our arrival on Utah Beach, we were assigned to *follow* General LeClerc. Unknown to higher command, LeClerc took a detour route through the Vosges Mountains that LeClerc had planned. In single file on the narrow mountainside road, we moved up the hill moving into Strasbourg the next morning taking the Germans by surprise. They were not expecting troops to come in over the steep, winding mountain for it was treacherous and a very narrow road to bring tanks and artillery over. It was raining. We always drove blackout at night, but headlights were made necessary because of the weather conditions to master the Vosges' narrow, steep winding road. They were transient appearance of partly subdued small light that could faintly be seen driving bumper to bumper, a *Shepherd for us drivers.* While crossing the Vosges, we soldiers of Service Battery were totally unaware that we were lost from the rest of the Battalion until reading John Eberhardt's "The Crossing of The Vosges". We were never told.

The Germans had a garrison of 15,000 men in Strasbourg. It was here the 250th Artillery Battalion fired a heavy barrage of ammunition across the Rhine River so the Germans couldn't destroy the bridge. The Rhine River is wide and powerful; flowing through deep gorges, steep high banks with granite cliffs, and one of the longest rivers in Europe. The French Government gave our Artillery Battalion the Brigade Citation.

The 250th was the first American unit to get to the Rhine River. General Eisenhower decided against the 7th Army crossing and directed General Patch toward the Saverne. A continuation of the Vosges type terrain; it was so cold! The cold was so biting it hurt, plus, there was heavy snow to contend with. The 7th Army would never get credit for getting to the Rhine River first. On March 26, General Haislip crossed the Rhine with the XV Corps at Worms to be sent south and east of Frankfurt; we would cross again on the Main River moving in a north-easterly direction.

I drove a lot, for Parks didn't like or want to drive. He was what you could call an *adventurous pioneer* of driving. Parks always wore his hat cocked to the side; a person that always had a smile. A chain smoker—I am sure I didn't help his health any by giving him my cigarettes. Ed Nida and I did all the driving. I was driving when we crossed the Danube River. It was the most beautiful river in Europe. It was here where we saw Hitler's famous "Autobahn" super highway that had been built just for his planned war. It was a multi-lane highway that stretched through Herford, Hanover, Braunschwig and Magdeberg, all led to Berlin. Others ran north and south thoughout Germany with on and off ramps.

As the battalion crossed France and Germany we were assigned to private homes at different times. I remember they would have these feather comforters that were 4-5 inches thick. They were sure warm. There was a lot of fraternization going on all the time. It is hard not to give to a little child when we had chocolate bars and them asking, "Please, choc-a-lot", or a stick of chewing gum.

The Dachau horror—no one could forget the horrid, gruesome sight. It still haunts those of us that saw the sight. The days I spent there before I was moved on were the worst days of my life! It left an indelible impression with all of us. Many thousands died of typhus after Dachau was liberated for the camp conditions were so horrible; the prisoners were unable to bathe and suffered from extreme malnutrition and fifth. Prisoners were used for such awful experiments. There were thousands of emaciated corpses to be buried. By any humane standards, captured German soldiers were never abused that way by the

Allied. We were not *Dum-kops*—as called by Germans meaning Dumbbell!

As a medic I experienced some funny things—some not so funny! I remember the day Charley Johnson with Service Battery was injured. Antiaircraft fell and hit his femoral artillery. It was on March 14, 1945 in Rahling, France-Bitche Fort area. It was pretty frightening for his injury was serious. I attended to the injury as I had been trained until the ambulance got there some forty minutes later. Charley had lost a lot of blood and was about to go into shock. I was not there when it happened but Jeff Adair was.

Sometimes it could be so quiet! At times you could hear the sound of artillery fire or see the flash. These times would put you in mind of home, or should I say: cause to remember. It is difficult to delineate like a nightmare, with the dawn.

General Patton, Patch and LeClerc never lived to see the effectuated results of their tireless work. All three had seen battle during World War I. Gen. Patton was in a car accident and died a few weeks later in Dec. 1945. General Patch died of pneumonia, exhaustion and surely a broken heart in Nov. 1945. Patch's only son, a West Point graduate, also, was killed under the command of his father in the Lorraine. His was buried in Epinal, France he served with the 79th Inf. Div., command by both Patton and Patch. Young Patch was under Patton when first injured. General Patch didn't know until he read it in the paper that his son had been injured. Patch located him in a hospital in England and had him brought to where he was to recuperate. During his recuperating the 79th & 90th Inf. Divisions and Haislip's XV Corps, to which the 250th was attached, were reassigned to General Patch's 7th Army on September 27, 1944. General Patch had landed on the beaches of Southern France on Aug. 28, 1944 and headed toward the Vosges. Young "Mac" had returned to duty just a few days when he was killed. General LeClerc was killed in an airplane sometime after VE-Day.

Our Battalion was sent back and forth supporting different divisions playing a dramatic role in many operations in Europe. The 250th helped the 3rd Infantry Division set a record. They fired more rounds on a given day than was ever fired by an Infantry Division. We spent quite a bit of time following the 3rd and 45th

Divisions after we were assigned to General Patch. The two veteran divisions came up from Southern France with General Patch. After our reassignment, we would stay with General Patch's 7th Army the rest of the time until after VE-Day on May 8, 1945.

The 250th Battalion with Haislip's XV Corps last leg of combat journey moved them toward the Alps on the left. On the 27th, the XV Corps were assigned with the 20th Armored Division. The 45th and 42nd Infantry Divisions were clearing a pathway for the armor into Munich approaching from the northwest. The 250th were on the outskirts. The Infantry were ready after the horror that was found at Dachau north and west of Munich. It was an experience that chills one to the bone thinking about it. One can never forget the tangled bodies adjoining the cremation furnaces, corpse-laden freight cars with emaciated bodies in grey-striped prison clothing. There was the mass gas chamber disguised as a shower bath (*Brausebad*) lure. Everyone was horror-struck with dismay. The SS Troops were ruthless!

The European War ended on the 7th Army segment at Munich. As ordered, General Patch would drive on for Salzburg, Austria, the last stronghold of the Nazis dictatorship. For the 250th Battalion, Salzburg was a welcome sight after a strenuous combat. A part of history the 250th took part in that didn't make the history books! The Seventh Army was a forgotten army that won, but went virtually unnoticed. General Patch worked laboriously, quietly doing his job. He never cared for the spotlight. The forgotten army would years later win another victory in the Gulf War in 1991 ... this time with some notice.

While assigned in Austria the 250th was split into two groups. I was transferred to the 975th Field Artillery Battalion, 90th Division and the 358th Infantry under the capable hands of Major Fuller. Sometime later, Major Fuller would make Colonel—well deserved!

Salzburg located in the foothills of the Bavarian Alps; a center for culture and music. I was assigned to a beautiful resort town, Mattsee, about twenty miles from Grodig, Austria. It was a very relaxing area.

I felt close to the men that were under my care. I gave a lot of shots, but I never looked forward to the monthly *short arm inspection*. As for myself—I was ill twice to any degree. I had the flu while at Plzeň, Czechoslovakia as I was being departed for home, and while stationed in England I got the mumps. I spent some time in the hospital there. Those mumps were no fun!

I was sent to Plzeň, Czechoslovakia from Salzburg to Marseilles and then I was put on a small Liberty ship that moved slowly up the estuary from the North Sea coming home. While on ship I assisted Dr. Anderson from Georgia.

The 250th Field Artillery Battalion was a special battalion that saw fear and oppression together as brothers. Brothers that gave purely; each were guided by a high sense of honor and duty with the best of command. It is hard to relive the events as they unfolded, day by day, week by week—after so many years. They are relived through literature, music, movies and paintings, but it is not simply an account as the events really happened. Without a doubt, the time I spent with the 250th Battalion have had a long lasting effect on my life as it has those I served with. We each appreciate and looked at the country we love differently. We each saw and experienced a lot, but we each were fortunate to be sent to European Theater rather than the Pacific Theater.

Medics were classified as noncombatants under the Geneva Convention so they did not receive combat pay, which amounted to an extra ten dollars a month, even though they faced the same dangers, they went through the same training, except for weaponry, as the men in the line company. Medics were not trained to use a gun at Camp Robinson. I did have training to use a 75mm howitzer in ROTC at Purdue University.

Medics had to be in good shape. Medics would be on call 24-7. They had no KP or guard duties. The medic being a neutral—meant protected by the Geneva Convention and denied the right to carry a gun, yet, the medics were strafed at. There were some medics who were captured, wounded and killed. The Japanese forces regarded medics as targets, resulting in our Allied medics covering or removing their insignia and carrying weapons for protection. In Europe, we medics removed our insignia and Red Cross band.

On October 30th, 1943, the first night with the 7th Army, our battalion was fired at. There were no casualties, but the medic command post was demolished by a direct hit with 170mm shells. Dr. Kohanek would play cards at night with some of the men. If it had been a little later it would have been a different story; no one had retired for the evening. Kohanek's sleeping bag had a piece of shrapnel through it. Thank God for the foxholes that had been dug earlier. There were some outrageous violations that occurred in both European and Pacific Theaters.

A Scottish scientist discovered penicillin (miracle drug saved countless soldiers) in 1928. It was an important technological breakthrough along with the prevention of disease for the Medical Department in World War II. Sulfanilamide (wounds), Atabrine (malaria), Morphine (pain killer) and Blood Plasma were greatly used and affected mortality in World War II. Sodium Amytal was used as a calming pill to the soldiers who suffered fatigue, but most cases it was to induce sleep. The soldiers called the blue pill "Blue 88 or Blue Dream".

Medical soldiers were trained to work as part of a team or unit, trained to perform *special duties* in a multitude of medical units in a chain of evacuation stretching from the frontlines to general hospitals in the Zone of Interior. All medical soldiers had to be acquainted with a body of medical and military knowledge basic to their training. Despite their status as noncombatants, medical soldiers had to be trained to protect themselves, their units, and their patients by Medical Replacement Center. The medical department is often overlooked as a contributing factor to the Allied success, but Medical Corps deserved as much credit for the Allied victory as any other units. It took *all units* from the top to the bottom to win the war.

The Medical Detachment enlisted men that served the 250th Battalion: Lloyd E. Thalacher, Herbert H. Porter, Harold Myers, William J. Kilgus, Dan Landrem, Dale E. Ashlock, Gilbert Gamez, Robert F. Hollinger, Roger L. Livermore, Joseph K. Welsh and myself. Captain Joseph M. Kochanek, Battalion Surgeon. Due to yellow jaundice, Welsh had to be left behind in a New York hospital. He was replaced by Loras J. Powers.

I wrote Carl's experience as a medic in 2004: "World War II Medic— European Theater".

*A fall day in France—1944: Carl Gwin was watering the cows just as he did back home on the farm.
A rare picture (not too clear) that Lecile Wix took of Carl with his medic band on*

L–R: Fred Bush, Howard Clanton & Dick Adair are wearing their German Lugar's

HOWARD CLANTON

SERVICE BATTERY: TRUCK DRIVER-RATION SUPPLIES

I was inducted into the army in 1943 at Fort Sill, Oklahoma—an artillery camp where I spent three days. Then, there was a group of us sent to Paris, Texas at a new camp called Camp Maxey where I was assigned to Service Battery. The first day there 1st Sgt. Christy came in the barracks and asked, "Is there anyone here that can drive a 2½ ton truck?" There were about 100 of us fellows in there. No one said anything. In the army everyone were told—not to volunteer for anything! I finally spoke up and said, "I can drive that truck!" There were 4-5 of us guys I was talking with and they laughed and said, "Sucker! Sucker!" Sgt. Christy said, "Soldier come with me." He got a hold of Sgt. Lecile Wix at the motor pool and got a truck and we drove over to the commissary. There were 500 hundred people there to be fed. We went to the rations area and came back after we got the food supplies loaded so everyone could be fed.

When I first started driving the supply truck there was a little Spanish boy helping. He took ill suddenly and was taken to the hospital where he passed away. That was when Fred Bush was assigned to Ration Supply. Dick Adair came in later. Dick and his brother, Jeff, came in at the same time.

While in France, I saw this old German tank sitting—you know how nosy Americans are? I started messing around looking down in the tank and saw a radio. There was a fella with Service Battery that had worked in a radio shop back home. I asked him if he could take the radio out and put it in the 2½ ton truck and he said, "Why, Yah! It has a little speaker and I will need something to mount it in." I said, "Well, we issue rations and I can get a cigar box." It worked perfect—we sure got a lot of good out of that radio. Ole Fred would listen to that classical music out of London. I said, "You don't like that music?" Fred said, "Yes, I do!" He was a Jewish boy from Chicago and he would go to all those classical concerts. I, myself, didn't understand or care for it. We listened to the Glenn Miller concerts broadcast at noon and Tokyo Rose for good music. Tokyo Rose would play Glenn Miller, Tommy Dorsey, and Harry James ... what we called good stuff!

When we were moving around Paris we ran out of gasoline. In order for us to go after supplies we drained gasoline out of the other trucks to go back for supplies. Cooks had to drain gasoline to cook with.

Ole Fred Bush and I were talking and I told him that I had to go 60 miles to see a movie in Texas. He thought that was terrible, for all he had to do was go to a bus stop and take a bus. We had a different life style, but we got along good.

When we were around the Saverne-Bitche area, Captain High came in and said 10% from each battery would be sent to the infantry to replace the Battle of the Bulge casualties. I just knew I was going to be one of the 10% having had National Guard while in school. Dick and Fred were tent partners. They were very chummy—about like brothers. They said I talked about the Germans all night. They teased me the next day—you didn't sleep very well, did you? They said I rolled and tumbled all night. I really didn't like the war.

The next morning I saw the Battery Clerk, Babin, and said, "Come here, I want to ask you something." Babin said, "What do you want, Howard?" I said, "I know you can't tell me anything—just answer me yes or no! I want to know, do I have anything to worry about?" Babin said, "Oh, Howard, you know I can't tell you that!" I said, "Yes or no—do I have anything to worry about?" He said, "No—and walked on." I said, "*Swish* that is a relief!"

Black market was rampant. One day, Dick, Fred and I were breaking down the rations and had just finished. We were getting ready to leave when Major

Bavaro, Battalion Executive, came up and said, "You boys step back." He was looking for sugar and cartons of cigarettes. He started dumping the clothing out. When he got done ole Fred started to get back up in the truck. The Major said, "Don't get in yet!" The Major Bavaro took and put everything back the way it was. Ole Fred, Dick and I decided he was a pretty nice Joe.

Major Bavaro was a West Point graduate and very strict. He was just checking to make sure we were not black marketing. There were fellows sending a lot of money home to their wives on the black market. Major Bavaro was later transferred to the 961st Field Artillery Battalion. He was made Colonel. We would talk to the MPs and they told us they were watching everyday for those that were black marketing.

Colombo drove a command car, unless on a convoy, then he usually drove a jeep for Captain High. We would start out at the front, but Colombo drove so fast we'd end up at the back—like a traveling salesman left behind this little guy with a heavy foot.

Pretty close to the end of the war the battalion was moving pretty fast; ole Dick, Fred and I got lost for three days. We roamed around and on the third day we happened to see two or three jeeps and a command car at an old church with 5 steeples. We drove up to the church; there was a major from an armored division at the top looking out. Dick said, "I'll go in there and see what I can find out." Ole Dick came back and told us what they said, "Yah, go right down there by the autobahn the bridge is out, but you get off on a service road there and go about two miles to the right." I was just joking and said, "Do I have to go down there?" We drove down there and stopped to look at the map. I said, "Yah, this must be about right." All at once there was a machine gun over to the right that opened fired and hit the engine and went right under the seat. Ole Fred Bush was sitting in the middle; he was out over Dick before Dick could move. We three got out on the right side of the road ditch away from the direction of fire. There was a tarp used to cover the supplies. It was just riddled with holes.

The major saw what was going on and sent a lieutenant down in a jeep and he took us back to the church. Dick asked the major, "What are you trying to do, get us killed?" The major had the lieutenant take us to the battalion in the jeep. When the four of us came driving up in the jeep, here comes ole Jeff Adair running and grabbing his brother, Dick. You never saw so much hugging in your life! Cpl. Shapland said, "There was word out that two ration trucks had been captured and that ole Jeff was about to have a fit."

Not having the supply truck; Colonel Jealous said, "We've got to have that supply truck!" The truck was full of supplies for five days and I said, "Yes, sir!" He told us we could use a jeep and to borrow a half track and go back up there and bring the truck back. Ole Fred said, "I'm not going back up there!" Well, I said, "I'll go and drive it back."

When we got up there on the exit the truck wouldn't start. When the officer jumped in the truck he said, "I thought you said it was hot up here!" The ration truck had a winch that we had to unwind by hand to move the truck. Parks got the motor running and we were about finished when two Germans on the highway opened fire. Using the 30cal. machine gun mounted on the jeep, they were blown to pieces. We finally got the truck back and Colonel Jealous had his five days of supplies.

While in France and Germany we would stay in people's homes. Some were young folks and some were elderly. They didn't want to be around so they would go to the cellar when there was one. We never got much R&R.

One night, while still in France, we were in a field when some Germans opened fired on us. Everyone ran for cover to the truck or trailer. Officer Olshine made a beeline for it, for he said, "Howard, if they capture us they'll let you live." Olshine feared for his life as anyone would. Olshine was Jewish.

I wish I had kept a diary of all the miles I drove. I did all the driving. The decision I made volunteering as a driver of a 2½ ton supply ration's truck for 1st Sgt. Christy was the best decision I ever made. I didn't have to pull guard, KP or latrine duty. Those ole fellows that laughed at my volunteering saw me later said, "You ole lucky so-an-so!" That I was—I had made a decision that was against all the rules of an army man's belief.

Sgt. Wilbur D (top)

Bottom: L–R: Wilbur D Johnson & Jerome Glickman. Wilbur is holding "C" Battery's little friend, "Little GI Joe". Little Joe would eat and sleep with the gun crew; educated "toughness for life's challenges". Earl McDuffie is in the background. This picture is so touching, for it shows our soldier's human side.

*Motorcycle that Wilbur Johnson used (**posing as an MP**) to get other soldiers
through the area that required a pass. At one time, Wilbur actually was a State Trooper.*

Wilbur Johnson

250TH BATTALION C-BATTERY & UNITED STATES AIR FORCE

$\mathcal{S}$ixty years ago, I was only 21, now 81 and living in Sherwood, Arkansas. I came home in 1964 to put my years of service behind to move on with life. It wasn't until presently I was interviewed by a young fellow that brought much of World War II to the forefront.

I was in Washington, DC with an uncle of a college student in Conway, Arkansas, Gabe Gentry. I had given Gabe a walking tour and we were discussing World War II. Young Gabe's interest about World War II was intrigued by the idea that he had a primary source through me. It would be four years later young Gentry borrowed a camera and filmed and interviewed 40 veterans from different branches of service including, myself from Arkansas. He would have us veterans describe the war happenings in adjectives, not text-book terms. He could ask: What did it sound like? What did it smell like? Gentry's oral project "World War II Remembered" is about veterans in Arkansas. He accomplished his intriguing piece of the nation's history, which was a motivation for him. He realized every time we lose a veteran, we lose a piece of history that is fading. This young fellow is to be commended for his sincere interest to see a part of history will stay intact by going to the real source—World War II veterans'!

The Arkansas Scottish Rite Freemasons, paid for the project to be done.

There have been 1,000 copies of the documentary printed and are to be donated to libraries and schools throughout Arkansas. There were 10 DVDs made.

I arrived in France in July, 1944 and fought for the next 297days without relief. General Patton, Patch and LeClerc kept on the move! I had forgotten, or should I say "repressed" the memory of shooting a German Captain until I read the short paragraph about history of my battalion. Either you kill them, or they kill you! You are just protecting yourself and fellow comrades.

In the southern part of England, where they had the range, the Germans would use those "Buzz Bombs" that were remote controlled. They were called "revenge" weapons, the V-1 and later the V-2 with no defense. They were deployed in early morning or at night, especially in foggy unclear weather.

It was in 1944 just before Thanksgiving, somewhere in the combat zone, C Battery Captain Glazer, two of my fellow comrades, and I went out on a reconnaissance mission to check on a reported enemy tank column late one evening. We topped a rise and surprised 26 or so German Soldiers about 100 yards on down the road. The captain shot at us; I aimed my M-I and fired killing him. The other German soldiers apparently in fear of there being reinforcement troops surrendered. The reconnaissance unit was lucky, because we were outnumbered by six to one. The Germans were evidently ready to surrender or they thought the Americans were an advance party of a superior force. I have a compass 3½ by 2½ that I kept in the worn, black, metal covered case that belong to the German Captain. The compass is quite accurate yet to this day.

Once while in mess line, the cooks were using a flashlight to see what they were doing. There was a fella that couldn't find his mess kit, so they started looking at the serial number on each and found two German soldiers in the line. They were after food.

The memories that veterans recalled from 60 years ago, don't make the history books. Stories of tedium to transfix and hold one spellbound with a command of interest to turning into perilous luring of danger.

One day, when my good buddy, Lindel McCullough saw a movement off in an island area. Lindel said, "If it is a hog, I'm going to kill it!" We made out for the area in a leaky boat. I was the bailer dipper while my good buddy was busy rowing. Sure enough it was a hog! We killed it and took it back and presented it to Sgt. Palmer who wanted nothing to do with it. He said, "It might be diseased!" When we told Captain Glazer, his response was, "What!" We told him, "It has to be government inspected." Glazer said, "I can take care of that!" The Captain found a red-ink pin and marked U.S. inspected. He then ordered, "Tell him to cook it, or I'm going to court-martial him!" Of course, Lindel wanted a hog feast—we got one!

It was nothing for us soldiers to go out searching for food—something we all done. It was good to have something different to eat. I remember one time a few of us went on a journey in search of eggs. We exchanged a rifle for a pitchfork and went to scout in the side-shed. I jabbed the fork into a pile of hay to pull myself up, which to my surprise I jabbed a German soldier in the buttocks. I sure got him moving! There were two of them. We found their guns later. Our hunt got us two German soldiers, but no eggs!

Yet on another day, a captain's driver scattered straw over the snow before pitching the tent and set a heater inside. The tent caught fire. The captain was angry, threatened court-martial. During the night there was a shell that landed and exploded where his tent had been. The next morning, he said, "Forget the court-martial!" This was one time where a mistake paid off.

There was a little boy 6-7 that spent about two years with C-Battery. He went everywhere with us. Lindel ask him one day where his mother was and he said, "The Germans took her!" He was happy with us men and stayed mostly with the gun crew where he slept and ate the same food we did. At first, he spoke no English. When you would see him he would say, "Hi, Joe!" He was called "Little GI Joe". When the battalion got to Austria, the men hired a Swedish lady to make him an army uniform, using their clothes and had stripes put on it. He had long, blond, curly hair.

After the war, we were assigned in Salzburg, Austria we couldn't leave out of certain areas. I found an old motorcycle and turned it in for a new one. Then I went to the motor pool and got some stencil that were used for the vehicles and stenciled MP on a helmet and armband. There was a shortage of MPs and the infantry was used at check points. I got where I could go up there and go anywhere I wanted—huh, they thought I was the boss and would ask me questions about things. The GIs would go anywhere they could, that was one of the reasons for the check points.

We were hauling soldiers back to Ulm, Germany city in South Germany in East Baden-Württemberg in a truck convoy. We happened to see a brewery and noticed it was still operational. There was a fella I kept with me that was an American-German with the named, Starr. He spoke fluent German. We went in to check the brewery out to see what it would take to get beer. You'd find old German marks (German currency) that weren't any good for anything, but found we could use them to buy beer. Our Commanding Officer would let us go get a truck load of old German marked beer (Snap Cap Beer) that had the stoppers! The men would get where they were wasting it. They would get a bottle and let it get warm and then go get another. We decided to start charging a nickel each. We took the money to the CO, but they wanted nothing to do with it and said, "You want to get me in trouble!" With that—we decided we could take the money and get a load of wine in Italy.

Once the battery was assigned to a Club Living Quarters, gosh—we didn't want to leave there! There was a woman there that would do everything. She had two daughters that helped her. There was a large dance room and we'd have the battalion band to play. There was a fine little boy from our battery called, Joe Avalos, that played the guitar. He was a little Mexican; he would smile all the time and very polite. Joe would later lose his left arm while driving his car, a truck side-swiped his car cutting off his left arm that he had out of the window—tragic loss! He was a good guitarist.

There was a family that three of us from "C" Battery lived with in Salzburg, Austria. We shared the third floor; McCullough was one of the three. The Germans had taken their horses and equipment and they were unable to farm. After the war the Germans turned everything in. We fellows went to see what we could do to help them out. We got them three horses, wagon, hay and plow so they could farm their ground. They were so appreciative of it.

We were moving the rations up to Salzburg. Each Battery would send three trucks to the Quartermaster Depot, where the food rations, gas, clothing and ammo were kept. Our battery's first truck would go back to Battalion Headquarters to unload and go back and get in line for another load. We would get an extra load. We gave food to the people where we stayed.

There were the moment's of World War II that hadn't bothered me through the years—until recently. The Dachau horror—a grueling memory of Poles and Jews found piled in boxcars, still lives with us soldiers that saw the sight the day Dachau was liberated. The diseases, starvation, and the torture would become a nightmare. Many soldiers would pay a high price for their heroic efforts for victory. The 250th Battalion lost some. It was deployed with 580 men. There were casualties from our battalion but the actual number is not known for some men had been transferred out; some were killed at the end of the war.

The 250th Battalion men were competitors, we wanted to be winners—that we were!

After the war, the Captain asked Wilbur if he wanted to enlist in Reserves for 18 months. They said they would send him to Oxford University in England free, and he would be made Staff Sergeant. However, Wilbur didn't want to go to college—he wanted to come home. He did take some college courses.

Wilbur returned to Arkansas, married and after nine months reenlisted into the Air Force. Wilbur spent a total of 21 years in the service. He served in Washington, Wyoming, Mississippi, Colorado, Texas, Alabama, and Alaska two years and in Europe three times in all. Wilbur retired in 1964 from San Antonia, Texas where he was in charge of the Air Police Town Control and Communications. Of all the places he was assigned he liked Cheyenne, Wyoming the best.

Wilbur was stationed at the Air Force Base at Little Rock, Arkansas for five years. His older brother, Elmer, had a "Motorcycle Escort" business as well as his enforcement job. Wilbur helped Elmer while he was stationed at Little Rock. There was a condition with being assigned on the base you were not suppose to wear a pistol. One day, the General saw Wilbur and later said, "Boy! Your brother and you sure look alike." He knew it was Wilbur. Later the General was giving an open house at the base and asked Wilbur if he could escort superiors (big wigs) around. Gee, Wilbur says, "I was most delighted to grant his wishes."

Elmer served in enforcement 19½ years. He was killed in an automobile accident a short time before his retirement.

Everett Wheeler

Everett Wheeler

HEADQUARTERS: PERSONNEL CLERK

*S*hortly after Everett graduated from high school he furthered his education at Parsons Business College, Kansas. Shortly before graduation from Parsons, he had an opportunity to take the Civil Service Examination. Everett would pass with flying colors. Soon he received an offer from the U.S. Corps of Engineers to work in their offices at Clearwater Dam, Piedmont, MO. January 1941 he was transferred to Norfork Dam and would marry a fellow college student, Virginia Reed in March. December 7, 1941, on a Sunday afternoon, Everett and Virginia went to the Morgan Drug Store for ice cream. The drug store was buzzing with the talk of "Day of Infamy"—Pearl Harbor. Everett would soon be transferred to Stuttgart, Arkansas, an air field for training glider pilots that was under construction. While there, he would receive a draft board call. He was an inductee from Arkansas, along with recruits from Oklahoma, Texas and Louisiana. They were all sent to Camp Maxey.

At Camp Maxey, Everett was assigned to Headquarters' Battery; everybody took cannonries practice–learning the basics of artillery. There was a year of in-tense training along with a month of maneuvers in Louisiana, then back to Camp Maxey to prepare for the AGF test. The 250th numerical score was the highest of any army artillery battalion at the time. This would come to the attention of General C. Patton. With fire power being vital for the European Theater victory, the 250th was put on alert to be sent from Camp Maxey to Camp Shanks, NY.

In February, 1944 the 250th was sail bound for England. In the middle of the Atlantic Ocean Everett would receive a message from Mother-in-law in Monett: BABY. Three weeks later Everett learned he had a precious baby girl, Janice. Three weeks would be a life time to hear *such* beautiful news.

In England, the battalion received further training stationed at Atherstone, England awaiting orders to cross the English Channel. The 250th were assigned to the 3rd Army, commanded by General Patton who personally had chosen the 250th Battalion.

The 250th shipped out of Southampton, England, on July 18, 1944 and arrived off the coast of France the next morning. Many vessels and other units were embarking there waiting for the weather to calm down. The battalion was unable to go to ashore until the 25th. Everett rode up to the assembly point in the back of a jeep—the battle for Normandy for the 250th Battalion had begun. The first sight for Everett; he saw a 1,000 of our Allied bombers heading for the front, plus their fighter escorts.

Along toward midnight someone hollered, "Gas" setting off a mad scramble for their gas masks. Many had been filled with cigarettes, candy bars, and other goodies issued just before they set sail. Many had been left in the trucks parked on the other side of the hedgerows. Those hedgerows were not easy to go through in the day, and almost impossible in the black of the night. It wasn't funny at the time, but the next day, when we got to comparing notes, it was hilarious.

General Patton's plan was to move to a major highway and secure one side, while pushing the German's out. With the support of the 250th Battalion and the relentless bombing by the Allied forces, the highway was secured. Then the battalion was assigned to the famed French 2nd Armored Division, commanded by General LeClerc. Because of the 250th battalion's speed of delivery firepower, General LeClerc called them his "Automatic Artillery".

Col. Jealous commander of the 250th Battalion asked General LeClerc where he wanted us to go, he replied, "Just get in line and follow us"—that we did! He usually was at the head of the column to Argentan and Nonant-Le-Pin where they went into firing position, shelling into the Falaise-Argentan Gap where most of the German Army was trapped and trying to get out. The Personnel Section hadn't been provided any transportation. We would have to hitch rides with whoever—usually the kitchen or ammo trucks. After the Falaise Gap firing ceased, two Motor Sergeants ventured into the gap where there was German equipment that had been abandoned and destroyed. They found a truck and drove it back. When a star had been painted on the doors and "USA" on the canvas tarp, it proved to be good transportation.

Everett recalls some names of the towns the 250th followed General LeClerc through: Vittel, Contrexeville, Dompaire, Epinal, Luneville and Nancy. There was a lot of rain, fog to content with. Everett said, "I thought since we were in a more or less open spot that I should dig a good foxhole. The ground was so saturated that the hole was soon filled with water—so that was the end of that!"

On Thanksgiving Day in 1944, the main force of the French Army, accompanied by the 250th entered Strasbourg. The Germans were taken by surprised and surrendered the entire garrison. The Germans would later blow up the Rhine River Bridge. The Battalion would take up position and begin interdictory fire on a crossroad at Kehi, Germany, and became the first American ground troops to fire into Germany. It was an action that the 250th along with the French 2nd Armored was awarded the Presidential Unit Citation.

General LeClerc considered the 250th Battalion so much an integral part of his army that he awarded their prized "Cross of Lorraine" emblem. It was around Strasbourg the 250th would be relieved from the French 2nd Armored Division and reassigned to an US Divisions for the rest of the war. We shelled Bitche, and then moved up near Luxemburg to the French town Rhaling about the time of the Battle of the Bulge was going on.

The middle of March, 1944, the final assault started, we crossed the Rhine River on a pontoon bridge at Worms; then crossed the Main River under a smoke screen on a pontoon bridge, skirted Nuremburg and seemingly were headed right for Dachau and Munich. At the time, the 250th was attached to the 45th Infantry Division of the Seventh Army. On April 28, the 250th was released from the 45th Infantry, and then on April 29th, Colonel Felix L. Sparks and the 157, 3rd Infantry Regiment and the 45th liberated the "Death Camp" at Dachau.

All units witnessed the unspeakable condition at Dachau. There were emaciated, scantily clad corpses everywhere. Stacked like cordwood to be thrown in the incinerator.

On May 7th, while in Salzburg, Austria word came that the war is over. The 250th was officially disbanded and members were transferred to other units. Some would serve in the South Pacific, other returned to the states.

Everett arrived at New York Harbor on November 11, 1945 on a dreary, foggy day, but home with a T/4 rank. Everett was discharged on November 24, 1945.

In 1979, members of the 250th traveled to Europe for the 35th Anniversary of D-Day. Everett recalled, "We spent some wonderful days visiting sights of London and Atherstone, where we had dinner with the mayor at the time. The 250th members presented the city with a memorial plaque. We attended celebrations at both Omaha and Utah Beaches, visited the Argentan-Falaise Gap area, and then on to Paris where the 2nd French Armored Division held a banquet in the 250th Battalions' honor." Next they visited Strasbourg where they presented the mayor with a plaque commemorating their visit 35 years earlier. They went on into Germany, visiting familiar sights along the way and ending their trip at Salzburg—where it had ended for the European Theater War.

For Everett, the reunions were something special! Not even the trip would compare to being with his fellow comrades and their family. Everett was the national coordinator for the 250th Field Artillery Battalion Group for 24 years. He was one of the major forces of the 250th Reunion. Everett lived knowing hard work and hard times during the Great Depression. He would jump at the chance to join the Civil Conservation Corps—President Roosevelt's civilian army to battle poverty while conserving natural resources. He would send home $25 of the $30 a month that he made to his mother. Everett would work himself through Business College. Carl and I never got to really know Everett and Virginia—that we regret! His presence shall be gone, but never forgotten....

Everett Wheeler, 91, of Mountain Home, Arkansas, passed way on April 25, 2005. The story I revised from an article in "The Baxter Bulletin", Mountain Home, Arkansas newspaper; furnished by daughter, Janice Harris. In 2006 I wrote Everett's Autobiography: Kansas Boy Stretches Horizons. He had written sixteen pages of his life's story that I was able to use. His book was easy to write, for I love history. I found Everett was *all about history*.

Virginia Wheeler

Janice Harris took me personally to present the book "Kansas Boy Stretches Horizons" to her mother, Virginia Wheeler. It was such a memorable time—thanks to Janice for taking me to see her mother, Virginia, so I could share that *special* moment in time. It was truly very touching.

Charles Wade, (photo left), standing in front of Baron's Chateau at Glanegg, Austria with John Gerken of Louisiana. Picture was taken at the end of the war. The camera used was borrowed from the Baron.

Charles Wade, Jr.

HEADQUARTERS' BATTERY:
COMMUNICATIONS & SWITCH BOARD OPERATOR

I was inducted into the army at Little Rock, Arkansas, and from there I was sent to Camp Maxey, Paris Texas for basic training. I served with Headquarters' Battery mainly in wire section and set communications. We'd lay wire to the battery and gun sections. We were moving all the time. If we had the time we would pick up the wire and reuse it. Toward the end of the war, I worked as switch board operator most of the time. There were times I would talk with the generals. I saw General LeClerc a couple of times in his jeep.

I was riding with Ralph Phillips when the 250th passed around Paris. The men that road in the truck, their faces sure got burned. I lucked out, for I got to ride in a jeep! Ralph was with B-Battery with the "Airplane Section" and worked closely with 2nd Lt. Richard Toolan. Lieutenant Toolan was one of the battalion's liaison pilots along with Lt. Cozort.

The battalion would serve with the 3rd and the 45th Infantry Divisions that came up from southern France with General Patch. The 3rd Army and the 7th Army met close to Dompaire. The 250th Field Artillery Battalion was reassigned from General Patton to the command of General Patch in the Lunéville area. We would stay under General Patch's command until after VE-Day.

One day, I was chopping wood when a US B-17 went over. It was crippled and you could see our men bailing out. The plane turned and came back—I went for cover! We were near a Maginot Line; a heavy fortified area that was lined with pill-boxes entanglements and anti-tank obstacles. Behind them lay a line of larger concrete casements and anti-tank ditches.

I made two rings out of the nuts from the bolts of the B-17 and a case using two 75mm shells and a 50 caliber shell for the handle. Some of the men retrieved machine guns from the plane.

In an area I can't recall, but some of us went in for some R&R. It was a small town and when we went back the Germans started shelling at us. We had no place to go; digging a hole was a fruitless task, for it'd fill with water. Nobody was advancing and we were next to a road, which was a good place to be.

At Dachau, Headquarters' Medics along with the rest of us went for shelter when a Junkers JU87—better known "Stuka" went over. A Stuka is a German two-seater dive bomber and close support aircraft. It was one of the most famous war planes of war history.

In the cellar where the medics had gone to get out of harm's way for shelter they brought out two German soldiers and guns. That Stuka sent everyone scrambling for cover. We were in around the area for a couple days. I went out the second day in the woods and shot a deer and upon my looking closer I saw a bunch of German aircraft; Jet planes as well as light bombers sitting there in the woods. It was something to see those Jets up close. They looked just like a big catfish. Their Me 262 Jets were superior to ours.

It was while we were at Dachau I got 6-SS swords, 1 rifle, officer's tent and several purses. I got authorization that day to send them home.

While still in the area, Arthur Goe said, "Charles, come go with me, for I want you to see something." The Dachau horror was so bad: there was bones in the crematorium; rooms had bodies stacked 8/10 ft. high and boxcars of bodies. We were only about 15 miles from Munich—the battalion's next move. It was there that would be the last battle for the 7th Army and the last for the 250th Field Artillery Battalion. We had spent 297 consecutive days with good field commanders' General Patton, General Patch and General LeClerc ... now it was

OVER. VE-Day was declared on the 7th of May, while the 250th was assigned in Austria. Headquarters and Headquarters' Battery men were assigned to a castle at Glanegg. The 250th Battalion was split up into two different groups. I was sent to the 975th Field Artillery Battalion under Major Fuller. Major Fuller was a West Point graduate and would later be made Colonel. The 250th Battalion fellow comrades bonded—learning to never take freedom for granted.

Peter Q. Cagle

PETER CAGLE

SERVICE BATTERY: MESS SERGEANT

*P*eter enlisted and entered the Army in January 1941. He left out from Ft. Jackson, South Carolina, and was sent to Fort Sills, Oklahoma. While at Fort Sills he was sent to a Bakers' School as Tech/Sgt. Peter said, "I thought my school days were over." Later he was promoted to Staff Sergeant, which meant more schooling. From Fort Sills Peter was sent to the new camp in Paris, Texas, called Camp Maxey, and assigned to the 250th Battalion.

The 250th Battalion shipped out from the New York Port on the Dominion Monarch for England. The Atlantic Ocean was rough and Peter was sick all the way. They arrived in Liverpool, England and from there they were transported by train to Atherstone, England where they were assigned to the Third Army commanded by General C. Patton.

While in England, Peter would meet and visit with his brother, Everett, who also was serving in the east.

From Southampton, England the 250th boarded the U.S.S. Herkimer for Normandy, France. Upon their arrival at Utah Beach they had to wait on ship for the sea to calm. The men were given Hershey bars—along with the cigarettes and other items. Peter got so sick while on the water he never did eat another chocolate (Hershey) bar.

Peter and Evelyn would have a baby daughter while he was stationed overseas. He sent a letter home saying, "I know it is time for the baby—can't wait to find out what it is." It would be 20 days before he received word that he had a baby girl born June 5th—day before D-Day.

At a reunion Ed Nida and Evelyn were talking. He said, "One time when a German airplane went over dropping bombs Peter made a quick dive for a frozen lake." Peter recalled when you was lying on the ground at night; you could fill the ground quiver. The war made Peter nervous.

Peter felt the time the 250th Battalion was out of gas outside of Paris, that the Germans were stupid and said, "For they could have overrun us." The Germans were obviously unaware of the situation.

As the Service Battery Mess Sergeant, he would always see that the men had hot food when it was possible. He had been ordered to dump the hot food out after the men ate, but Peter responded, "Sir, let me tell you something— you can court marshal me or do what ever you want, but I can't stand to see these children going hungry!" Food was given to the French children standing around.

In France, Peter said, "We would go out in the countryside and the French would give or we would pay for eggs and potatoes to fix to eat."

Peter brought home several "Stars and Stripes" army newspapers. In one it said, "The 250th alongside the 45th Infantry fired their last shot of the war at Munich."

Peter came home by way of airplane into Florida on a Sunday morning, then onto Old Fort Gordon, in Augusta, Georgia. He returned home with his nerves just shot. He said, "Dachau was the most awful sight I had ever seen—seeing the crematorium and the smell of human flesh." It defiantly wasn't a scenic sight, but a horrifying tale that no one wanted to tell!

Evelyn Cagle was so pleasant to work with for Peter's story by phone. He passed away in 2001. Peter received a Bronze Star for his dedication—something he was proud of! A Bronze Star was engraved on his monument.

J.D. Duncan

J. D. DUNCAN

HEADQUARTERS' BATTERY

I was drafted on December 28, 1942 and reported for service on January 12, 1943 at Gravette, Arkansas, and sent to Camp Robinson, Arkansas. From Camp Robinson I was sent to Camp Maxey, Paris, Texas were the 250th Battalion was organized as a non-divisional 105mm Towed Howitzer Battalion. It would be my first series of training courses to be a soldier. It was an excellent camp with good training facilities. I was assigned to Headquarters.

We were sent to Louisiana for maneuvers and then back to Camp Maxey. They were getting us ready for overseas duty. We would depart from Camp Maxey and was sent to Camp Shanks, New Jersey. We shipped out from the New York Harbor on the Dominion Monarch, a slow moving ship, crossing the North Atlantic for Liverpool, England. On July 1944 we left from Southampton, England where the 250th Battalion boarded the U.S.S. Herkimer for Normandy, France. We arrived off the coast of Normandy, France at Utah Beach. It would be where we would see our first real taste of war.

The 250th were first assigned with General Patton's 3rd Army, to be reassigned to the 7th Army, which was commanded by General Patch with whom we would spend the rest of the time until we were reassigned after VE-Day. Although, we saw combat battle—all I can say, "We had a good time!" We made the best out of a not-so-pleasant time. I became close to James LeBoeuf, Sedric Burnett and Warren Porche; all three are deceased. I worked as radio operator and truck driver to being a mechanic with Headquarters' Battery.

After the war, we were reassigned to Salzburg, Austria where the 250th Battalion men were reassigned to different areas. Headquarters' Battery was housed in the castle of Glanegg, Austria. In June 19, 1945 there were 10 of us Gehrkin, Lindahl, Bowman, Fritch, McDow, Bernardo, Carmichael, Greene, Kasten, Williams, Bazan and myself from Headquarters' Battery took a furlough to Nice, France on the Riviera. We returned on July 1, 1945 and found the 250th Battalion splitting up. I was transferred to the 975th Field Artillery until I received notice I had points to go home. I came home on the Liberty ship, returning to the New York Harbor where we were shipped out from on February 11, 1944. I got home on December 23, 1945; discharged at Fort Smith, Arkansas.

Standing L–R: James A. Leboeuf, J.D. Duncan and James Fortune.
Kneeling L–R: Warren Porche, Carl O. Biggs & Angelo R. Bernardo at Southampton, England—1944

Dr. Robert (Bob) Weaver

Dr. Robert J. Weaver

ARTILLERY C-BATTERY: EXECUTIVE OFFICER

I grew up in Burlington, Kansas where I went to grade and high school. While in high school I joined the 35th Division of the National Guard. It was a little before I was 18, so I had to tell them a little difference in my age. We had regular drills and so forth until summer camp of 1940 when they passed the draft law, Selective Service Act. We were called into federal service for what was supposed to be for a year's training. We were sent to Camp Robinson, Arkansas for my basic training, advanced training, and maneuvers until Pearl Harbor.

I had been in about a year when Pearl Harbor was bombed; Japanese attacks brought global war. Japanese planes destroyed the US fleet on December 7, 1941.

Two weeks after Pearl Harbor we were on a train headed west, we naturally thought we were on the road to the Pacific, but the train ended up in California. While in California, we did coastal defense up and down the coast from San Francisco down to San Diego and numerous places watching for submarines or a possible Japanese invasion for six months.

I left the division and went to OCS at Fort Sill, Artillery OSC; a candidate in which one is trained to become Officers, Second Lieutenants. I got a delay in route to Fort Sill which let me go through home. That's when I got engaged to Mae Kepler. I was at Fort Sill for three months. That's where they came up with the slogan of "Ninety Day Wonder!" Fort Sill was so hot it's a wonder as many lasted as long as they did.

Officer Candidate School was a school, class and practical, kind of like an outdoor lab a lot of time. There was a lot of pressure that they kept you under was what made it rough. Quite a number of men decided they were not going to do it and packed up and went home—by home; back to their old unit. Officers gave and received orders.

From Fort Sill I went to Camp Maxey, Texas to a separate artillery battalion. On our way we got another delay in route and that's when I went back by Burlington and Mae and I got married. I took Mae to Paris, Texas, with me. She stayed in Texas until we went overseas. Mae kept busy, the battalion commander's wife had a sewing circle that she got involved in and she became leader of a local Girl Scout troop there in Paris.

We went in just as cadre at Camp Maxey. The battalion was just in the organizing stage when we arrived. At Camp Maxey, I was first assigned with Service Battery, later to be transferred to C-Battery.

There were seventeen of us when we got out of OCS; we were commissioned as Second Lieutenants. All seventeen of us went to this one artillery battalion so it was kind of a close knit group. I was promoted to First Lieutenant in March '43. Just one month before I was twenty-one—still a kid!

In 1944 the battalion was sent to Europe. We left Texas in February of 1944. Embarkation in a convey crossing the Atlantic, on the Dominion Monarch ship landing in Liverpool, England. The 250th was the only battalion stationed at the little town called Atherstone. We were based there until the battalion went to Normandy. While at Atherstone there were continuous training and maneuvers.

On July 12, 1944, the 250th was officially relieved as guards of P.W.E. No. 7 at Swanwich, England. At 0618, July 17, 1944, the battalion moved to a marshalling area near Salisburg—Southern England's jumping off point to France. The staging area was merely a reserve area, until there was room to board troops on the waiting ships at Southampton, England. After five days aboard the LST U.S.S. Herkimer, the 250th landed on Utah Beach, Normandy, July 24, 1944.

We crossed the channel six weeks after D-Day on the U.S.S. Herkimer;

loaded with the necessary equipment. When we arrived at Utah Beach we had to wait on ship for the sea to calm. Then we moved a few miles inland. We were assigned to General Courtney Hodges' First Army until General Patton came in from England where he had been as a decoy. He surprised the Germans coming in from the west, for they had expected him to come from the east.

General Patton came from England arriving July 1st at Utah Beach and started his breakout at Saint Lo. We were attached to General (Jacqus) Leclerc's 2nd French Armored Division through the Argentan-Falaise gap. There were quite a lot of German soldiers and dead horses. The Germans were still using horse-drawn artillery. Even after they had equipment for blitzkriegs; war conducted with great speed and force and mechanized ground forces in close coordination, and all that type of thing.

There were four guns to a battery, and when we went into position, we were given a compass (azimuth) to lay the guns or point them on. Then we put that in the center of the field of fire and guns would be lined up in a row—not behind one another. And then fire from there. It'd take ten or fifteen minutes to get the guns into position. They were light enough that they could be moved around by hand. They unhooked from the prime mover or the truck. The gun crew would set up in position and the forward observer or fire direction center would tell you where the target was. We did quite a lot of night firing all through the campaign. Sometimes there would be feedback whether you were close to your target or off your target. Depending on where the target information was coming from. A forward observer would report back. Their report would affect whether the target was destroyed or whether there was a need for more firing. Sometimes target orders came from headquarters in what they called a *TOT* or "time on target." Gunners would be given a certain azimuth and location, direction and elevation to fire and the exact minute to fire. It came from the fire direction centers. We rarely ever knew what our target was. It was timed so that all of the artillery in the division, or the corps sometimes, would all land on one target at one time. From what information we received, the German soldiers thought that was the most devastating of any fire that they had to come in on them. The targets could be a column of vehicles or a bivouac of German soldiers.

The forward observer sometimes would locate a machine gun for the target. Sometimes it wouldn't be much or quite a large target, such as a whole column of trucks on a road. On some of the TOT's, the whole corps artillery would fire on the same target with 105s, 155s up to the 240mm howitzers.

General Patton was commander of General Haislip's XV Corps that the 250th Field Artillery Battalion was assigned to. He was a top tactical officer who liked the spotlight. You didn't like him personally, but you didn't want to serve under anyone else. Everyone got reports from the Stars and Stripes and radios. Everyone knew Patton covered more ground, killed more enemy with fewer casualties than any other general in the business.

Our battalion was composed of five batteries, three firing batteries and a service battery and a headquarters' battery. We were a separate battalion attached to a division, composed of the various arms; the infantry in particular, was formed then into regiments and after they triangularized the divisions from the old square division of the National Guard days, there were three regiments in a division, plus all the support groups including the artillery in the support group. A corps was composed of several divisions plus the separate units. Then an Army like the 3rd Army was composed of several corps.

In the fall of September 1944, the 250th Battalion was giving artillery support to the XV Corps, a part of the 3rd Army, also working with the 208th Field Artillery group. There was a request to transport the 79th Infantry Division to the area of XV Corps. I commanded a convoy, leaving Troyes on September 7. On September 9th, the 79th Infantry was at the bridgehead at Dejonville. On the 10th, the 250th was ordered to rejoin the 2nd French Armored Division. Our battalion served as spearhead in supporting the armor.

In France Lt. LeRoy Schmidt got sick and was transferred out. I was then made Executive Officer.

The 250th Battalion went across France attached to the French Second Armored Division. Then when we got to about 15 miles west of Paris, they let them go on in to liberate Paris and sent the 250th and other attached troops in an arc around the south of Paris. We went to about 15 miles east of Paris and waited. We rejoined the French Armored after they came out and continued east.

We were very upset that we didn't get to go into Paris. We had fought with the French all the way, and then had to by-pass around Paris. For General Patton, his 3rd Army being denied the liberation of Paris was a disappointment.

I can't recall the exact locations. The 250th had several firing positions. Once while assigned with the French, we advanced a hundred miles one day. That was the biggest advance in a single day.

In Eastern France on September 1st, the 3rd Army ran out of gas. We drained the gas from all the other battery trucks to send the ration truck back for supplies. Drained gas was used to cook with. There wasn't anything Patton could do. He was forced to halt all combat movement; he couldn't move. If the Germans had broken through, we had just been sitting ducks. We were there a week until a gas supply was received.

General Patch's Seventh Army moved up the eastern side of France and joined the 3rd Army in Northern France. The two Armies met in a tank battle on a rolling countryside. General Eisenhower ordered the XV Corps to be transferred to General Patch's 7th Army. On September 27th, we were assigned to the Sixth Army group. We transferred September 28th a few miles northeast of Lunéville to the command of Lt. General Patch's Seventh Army, where we would spend the rest of the time until reassigned after the war. Corps assigned to the Seventh Army: XI, XXI and the XV, to which we were attached along with General Leclerc's 2nd French Armored Division, 3rd, 36th, 45th, 79th and the new 63rd and 71st Infantry Divisions. General Devers, commanded the 6th Army Group, to which the 7th Army belonged. The 79th and the 90th Infantry we had been with.

General Patton's 3rd Army worked north toward Bostogne—The Battle of the Bulge. We were in the Alsace area. The battalion fired in the Colmar Gap battle, and we went into Strasbourg, France on Thanksgiving Day of 1944. Part of the 250th Battalion stopped for a Thanksgiving Day dinner at 1130. We were served a turkey dinner that the field kitchen crew had prepared that evening in Strasbourg.

The 7th Army was the first to get to the Rhine. Our Battalion from the Strasbourg position fired the first American shell across the Rhine River into Germany. General Eisenhower decided against the 7th Army crossing the Rhine

River at that time. It would be about another three months after we had been in Strasbourg that the 7th Army would cross the Rhine at Worms to proceed on east.

There were a lot of prisoners of war, but in our position as a separate artillery battalion, we didn't have much contact with them. They were taken by the forward units, the infantry and the reconnaissance units, etc. and immediately shipped back. Before we went to Normandy, after the maneuvers in Southern England, we spent a few weeks up on the English/border guarding a prisoner of war camp that had been established. Many were processed to the United States.

I remember the night of 4th of July. It was bitter cold. Probably wouldn't have remembered it had it been any time except July. Those Germans had a lot of money and so forth. There were barrels filled with French francs. We didn't pay attention to them, didn't figure they were worth anything, just worthless paper. Not until we'd been on the continent for awhile did we learn that the pay would be with the same currency as the country we were serving in. I don't know whether the army used any of the money or not. But we were long gone from those barrels full when we realized that.

As the 7th Army continued east there were several firing positions into Munich. The 45th Infantry went into Dachau ahead of the 250th Battalion. Afterwards we were able to take our people in to see it the next morning. When the group I was with got there, there was still boxcars on the railroad siding. Most were stacked two feet deep with bodies. The gas chamber in the crematorium building had a stack of bodies in it about six feet high. The fires were still going in the crematorium ovens. It had been kept going right up to the minute that the Allied moved in.

The 45th Infantry moved ahead of the 250th into Munich, which they were ready for after Dachau. Upon our arrival there we saw total destruction from the bombing. The 250th Field Artillery took part in ending the war in Europe. The 250th Battalion fired their last rounds of the war in Munich on the Seventh Army segment.

We left Munich and were in a little town just south of Salzburg, Austria when V-E Day was going to be within minutes. After V-E Day we were assigned MP occupation duty in Salzburg. Captain Howard Leslie, A-Battery

Commander and I got orders to return home in the early part of September; our third wedding Anniversary. We had enough points to fly home, but we never did see an airplane. We came home on a Liberty ship. Came through New York and Fort Dix, New Jersey and then to Fort Leavenworth and I reached Topeka on the 20th of September. It had been nearly five years on active duty. The only time I ever reported on sick leave was one time out at Fort Ord, California when I got poison oak.

In 1979 the 250th reunion group went back and retraced the route of the battalion. We were entertained in Paris by the veterans of the 2nd French Armored Division. They had their separate club in Paris. There was a large turnout for the reunion. The widow of General LeClerc was there and she signed certificates. The certificates were from the President of the Republic of France, but she autographed them. The Mayor of Strasbourg gave us a card: a cathedral in Strasbourg in 1944—a thank you for liberating the city. It was given as a Christmas card.

When our battalion people were assigned different places during the war there was some resentment. However, there were others that were very cooperative. In Austria after the war, we'd be billeted to private homes; quite a number of people would open part of their houses. Yet, there were those that were inclined to resent us.

I remember the men in C-Battery having a little boy, but I can't tell you what he looked like. It was one of those–you knew, yet you didn't. There were things we Officers' were aware of, but we didn't always do anything about.

My final primary artillery assignment was as Battalion Commander of the 563rd Field Artillery Battalion 89th Division USAR, which was headquartered in Great Bend. Howard Leslie was at that time the Commander of another Field Artillery Battalion of the 89th Division USAR. I retired from the army reserve in 1960.

Most of Dr. Weaver's story came from his "World War II Experiences" of Dr. Robert J. "Bob" Weaver. Copies are at Dwight D. Eisenhower Presidential Library; American Legion Argonne Post No.180 in Great Bend, Kansas; and the National

Archives Central Plains Branch in Kansas City, Missouri. European Theater campaigns: Normandy, Northern France, Rhineland, Ardennes-Alsace and Central Europe. He received a Bronze Star for his meritorious service. Dr. Weaver is national coordinator for the 250th Reunion group ... a real contributor!

The next three pages are courtesy of Dr. and Mrs. Weaver. They are very interesting. As a portrait painter myself—I really like the (Merevale Park 1979 Atherstone, England) painting by Nell Pearson. Pictures are from their 250th Reunion Group that returned to France in 1979 to retrace their World War II movement across France.

Soldiers were not allowed cameras during the war, but as the war progress there was some easement on the picture taking. All restrictions were for security reasons.

Dr. Robert J. Weaver and his beloved Mae

MEREVALE PARK 1979 ATHERSTONE, ENGLAND

PICTURE: COURTESY OF DR. AND MRS. WEAVER

Le Président de la République,

Le Conseil des Ministres entendu,

Décrète :

La Dignité de Maréchal de France
est conférée à titre posthume, au Général
d'Armée Philippe, François, Marie
Leclerc de Hauteclocque

Fait à Paris, le 23 Août 1952.

V. Auriol

Par le Président de la République,
Le Président du Conseil des Ministres,

A. Pinay

Le Ministre de la Défense Nationale,

R. Mevey

Le Secrétaire d'État à la Guerre,

NOËL 1944

EN SOUVENIR DU 23 NOVEMBRE

MAIRE DE STRASBOURG

PICTURE: COURTESY OF DR. & MRS. WEAVER

Herbert (Herb) Olshine visiting England

Herbert Olshine

SERVICE BATTERY: AMMUNITION SUPPLY OFFICER

I was a member of the National Guard for 24 hours in Tennessee before my going into regular army in 1941. I was sent to Fort Sills, Oklahoma for three months for OCS: Officers' Candidate Training School. They trained survival, caring for yourself, as well as others. We even dismantled a jeep, for they wanted us prepared for the unexpected. I was assigned to the new 250th Field Artillery Battalion as Ammunition Supply Officer with Service Battery at Camp Maxey, Paris, Texas. I made sure the troops had the supplies needed and if not; we went to the supply depot and got them.

We left New York Port for overseas on a slow moving British luxury ship, Dominion Monarch on February 11, 1944. We left in the dark of night crossing the North Atlantic. It was a cold, rainy night mixed with sleet. We took the northern route, passed along the Irish Sea Coast and arrived February 23rd at Liverpool, England. The battalion was transferred to waiting trains that took us from Liverpool to Atherstone where we were billeted in a small British encampment area on the outskirts of Atherstone. The first night the battalion encountered several gas warnings alerts, which meant not much sleep.

While at Atherstone the 250th Battalion was transferred to the command of General Patton. General Patton was in Northern England as decoy while getting his Third Army ready for the Normandy invasion.

While at an artillery installation in Wales, England, on the morning of June 3rd, all officers and first three grades of non-commission officers went to hear Lt. General George Patton speak. In his rough talk he said, "I am going to teach you to take care of yourself, so the enemy won't sneak up on you with a bag of—and hit you over the head." I saw him one other time during shower time while overseas. He was there for inspection.

At Swanwich, England Service Battery was assigned to do guard duty for prisoners of war. The prisoners had been taken on June 6, 1944 D-Day. After about a month, the battalion moved July 17, 1944, to an area near Salisburg in Southern England to a reserved area until there was room to board troops on a waiting ship at Southampton, England. We boarded the LST (Landing ship tank) U.S.S. Herkimer and arrived on the Utah Beach, Normandy, July 23. As we approached Utah Beach, we saw a great deal of devastation. During July, other Third Army troops were continuously moving across the Channel and funneling through Utah Beach.

After we unloaded on the sandy beach, there was an introduction to a 35 mile road march. The first night there wasn't much sleep for the men; gas alerts, slit trenches were dug with German aircraft flying low, checking for troop locations. Until the arrival of General Patton, we were under the command of Lt. General Courtney Hodges of the First Army.

General Patton arrived from England surprising the Germans not coming in from the west, but east. Once there, he moved at a fast pace—not much time to recapture our thoughts.

I remember those hedgerows we went through—we'd get cut up. The hedgerows contoured around small fields that were irregular. Good defense for the Germans. Fighting in the hedgerows was terrible … they were something else! Hedgerows were so big and tall with thick brush on top; very dense. It was an area where the Germans used their wicked 88mm anti-aircraft and anti-tank weapon used as field artillery that was very accurate and used to great effect.

It was near Dompaire, on this rolling country terrain the 3rd Army and 7th Army would meet. The 250th Battalion transferred September 28th northeast of Lunéville to the command Lt. General "Sandy" Patch until after VE-Day. The 79th, 90th Infantry Division and General LeClerc's 2nd French Armored Division were also transferred to the 7th Army. The 250th had been assigned to General LeClerc at different times. He liked the 250th Battalions' support and called us his "automatic artillery".

The 250th Battalion had no special staff group consisting head of finance. Colonel Jealous would appoint an officer to act as finance officer, each pay day we officers rotated. It became my turn when we were in the thick of war. The payroll had built up. I took the payroll to Officer Herbert Glazer of C-Battery. He said, "I don't want that money!" Glazer's C-Battery men were shooting two different directions: north and south. So I put it in his jeep. I was gone about a half hour and went back. There was a lot of payroll there in Herbert's jeep, but he had gotten it and put it in a safe place.

The Dachau Concentration Camp thing was terrible! I was with the troops when we went there. Those who survived were so weak that they would fall backward trying to stand. It was just an awful sight to see. Many died later.

The war wound up in Salzburg, Austria. All through the war the Service Battery were with or close behind the battalion. Service Battery men worked untiring.

The 250th Battalion had two Majors. Major's Bavaro and Fuller were great contributors to the 250th Battalion. They were roommates at West Point. They both would become Colonels.

The 250th Battalion would take their last road march from Munich to Salzburg, Austria. They saw their last battle at Munich's outskirt where it all ended on the 7th Army segment commanded by General Patch. The war was over at 0241 hours in the morning hours on May 7, 1945, an unconditional surrender.

I got an opportunity later to go to Berchtesgaden—Hitler's infamous retreat "Eagle's Nest". It was located on the Alps Mountain side. The SS troops had set it afire as our Allied troops were moving in.

Service Battery was billeted to a hotel in a village at Grodig, Austria. The 250th Battalion would be reassigned after VE-Day. I was sent to the 975th Field Artillery Battalion.

Our battalion had good men, Officer, Colonels and Commanders; all which contributed to our succeeding with honor. The 250th Battalion completed 297 consecutive days in combat without relief.

Finally the day came, in December 1945 that I was on a small Liberty ship headed for home. The ship was of flimsy workmanship making the trip rough. We encountered storms and the trip was slow, but I was just happy to be coming HOME. By the grace of God, most of the battalion returned home. The nation's greatest war lasted three years, eight months, and seven days....

Officer Olshine served Service Battery men with care and respect despite the hardship of war. He served providing humanity at such an inhumane times; men away from their homeland (as he was) serving on foreign soil. He received a Bronze Star for his virtue shown. European Theater campaigns: Normandy, Northern France, Rhineland, Ardennse-Alsace and Central Europe. Service Battery's "beloved" Officer, Herbert Olshine, passed away February 25, 2005 at age 86. There was a private service. His story was done in December 2004-January 2005 for the book.

Herbert D. Glazer—March 2005

HERBERT D. GLAZER

"C" BATTERY COMMANDER

I was drafted into the Army in January 1942. I left Memphis for Camp Oglethorpe (south of Chattanooga, TN) where I had 6-8 weeks of basic training. I "took pictures of lungs" of the enlistees.

Next, I was sent to Ft. Bragg in South Carolina where I continued training for about 3-4 months before being sent to Officer Training Camp at Fort Sill, Oklahoma where I trained as a Field Artillery Officer. I remember when my brother Philip surprised me when he was sent there as well. We were able to see each other at Fort Sill for a couple of months.

My next assignment was a transfer to Camp Maxey in Paris, Texas where I had more intensive artillery training and where the 250th Field Artillery Battalion began. Here we practiced shooting guns and handling all artillery equipment. I was the Commanding Officer for Battery "C" which encompassed about 100 men. I stayed at Camp Maxey from August 1942 until the early part of January 1944.

In about January 1944, we shipped off to England on a Canadian Luxury ship which had been converted to a military style ship which housed, I think, several thousand men. This was about a 2 week trip; I was lucky as I was one of the few men who did not get seasick. I bet 2/3 on board got ill at some point or another.

We landed in Liverpool and from there we went on to a small town where we continued artillery training.

In about May, 1944, the Service Battery and the 250th Battalion headed to England near the Scottish border. Here we were responsible for some German POW's captured by other units in France.

We later moved into France in July (1944) where fighting between the Allies and the Germans was underway. General Patton took over our Battalion and the France 2nd Armored Division merged with ours. I remember being about 20 miles or so from Paris and being ordered not to go into the city; only the French armies could enter as Paris had been liberated and Americans were not allowed to share in their victory at that time.

Our assignment next was to move toward Berlin, which is what General Patton wanted, but our fuel resources ran out and we were delayed much to the General's dismay. I do remember one hot day taking a much-needed shower when lo and behold, close by me—also cleansing himself—was General Patton himself—with the rest of his men. He was a great military leader.

I also remember spending the night in the Vosges Mountains close to Strasbourg, and going down the mountains to capture Strasbourg.

One of my strongest recollections is when the 250th went outside of Munich in around April 1945. Hitler's Camp Dachau had just been liberated and we were amongst the first to view the "Displaced Persons" from this death camp. I remember bodies stacked up in open-air rail cars. I remember the crematories with smoke. I remember the ex-prisoners looking like skeletons and us not being able to offer them any of our excess food (due to an order that came down a few days later) because our food was making them sick. So we stopped. I also remember these freed ex-prisoners using the butts of German guns beating their guards and other German soldiers to death and no one intervening.

One interesting story I clearly recall is the one time I shot my 45 pistol. It was late one afternoon. We were looking for German gun locations and I saw a man in the distance lift his gun. Lucky for me I shot him first and I was told that the German victim had a large hole in his chest. I knew that if I had not shot him first, I would have been the one to take a bullet.

I also remember standing next to a young man from Blytheville, Arkansas.

We were close to a river where a bridge was in despair. He was in B-Battery. A nearby shell went off and he got hit and the next day he died. I didn't think it was a fatal wound at the time.

My men in Battery C, while at Camp Maxey, attached a nickname to me— *The Claw*—in other words, tough man. Well, I was tough. I had once read that you must train your artillerymen to be tough and levelheaded so they won't get scared under pressure. I tried to go by the book.

One more recollection is when I pulled the cord to fire the first shell over the Rhine River around March 1945. I pulled the cord so hard that I broke the cord.

My boat home in December 1945 was a "Liberty Ship". I was not with the 250th at the end of my war days; I had been transferred to a different unit so I returned home with different men.

Anyhow, on a rather funny note, to this day, I have always called myself "lucky" in various aspects of my life and luck was certainly with me during the many poker games I found myself involved with on that boat heading for home. However, I certainly would not have called myself lucky with poker on prior occasions but during the trip home I had pockets filled with IOU notes written by boys from all over the country. Small stakes, mind you, but I think if I had collected, I could have won several thousand dollars. However, I tore up all notes and told everyone "don't worry about it." We had left from the south of France and landed in Boston.

My years serving in World War II were tough but I gained valuable lessons that have been with me through the years.

Herbert was born and raised in Memphis, Tennessee. He had three brothers (Philip also served in World War II) and one sister. He attended public schools in Memphis, graduated from Humes High School in Memphis and went on to the University of Illinois, located at Champaign, Urbana as well as the University of Illinois School of Law where he graduated in 1936. Herbert is a very enjoyable to talk with–we have never met. Herbert told me he has only been sick twice in his life; once in college when his appendix ruptured and spent the month of February in the hospital. He said, "The good Lord has been good to me."

Byrd L. Lewis, (top): picture taken in Paris, France, while vacationing—1945

(bottom), Leroy and Lovetta Lewis, celebrating their 60th Anniversary —2007

Byrd L. Lewis

ARTILLERY B-BATTERY: RADIO OPERATOR & FORWARD OBSERVER

I have written a book entitled "Memories of My Experiences as an Artillery Soldier During World War II". It was copyrighted in 2001. I wrote it especially for my two grandsons Jonathan Lee Knight and Lance Taylor White. When they grow up and study World War II in high school and college, I want them to know the truth about the reason for World War II, the truth about the contribution made by the American people, and the truth about man's inhumanity to man. I want them to know the "awfulness" of war and the importance of peace. Also, I want them to know some of their grandfather's war experiences firsthand when they are old enough to understand more fully about World War.

The following is a short summary about the 250th and its trek across France and Germany without the unusual personal experiences that I related in my book.

The 250th was a truck drawn, 105 millimeter howitzer, field artillery battalion. An artillery battalion at the time was made up of five batteries. There were Headquarters, A, B, C, and Service batteries. Headquarters Battery, which consisted of the battalion commander and other battalion officers, was the location of our Fire Direction Center. A, B, and C were the three firing batteries, and each of these batteries had four 105mm howitzers. The fifth battery was Service Battery, which kept us in supplies of ammunition, gasoline, food, and water. We had a medical detachment with our battalion which consisted of a medical doctor, and twelve medics.

If I remember correctly, the 105mm howitzer had a very accurate range up to five miles and a fairly accurate range up to a maximum range of seven miles. This howitzer fired a 36 pond shell or projectile that was just over four inches in diameter and about eighteen or twenty inches long. When an artillery shell hits and explodes, it burst into hundreds or maybe thousands of jagged-edged pieces of shrapnel, which fly in every direction. Flying shrapnel is destructive and deadly!

When we recruits arrived at Camp Maxey, a newly built army camp ten miles north of Paris, Texas, our officers and noncommissioned officers were at the base waiting for us. The enlisted men in the five batteries of the 250th Field Artillery Battalion were from five states with approximately the same number of men from each state. The states were Oklahoma, Texas, Louisiana, Arkansas, and New York. At first, I thought about what an odd mixture we were. But, as time went on and we worked and trained together, we became one solid, well-prepared unit.

Our 105mm howitzer gun crews were firing on German targets that were usually anywhere from one mile to five miles in front of them. Therefore, they had to have forward observers to go up to the front lines to radio or telephone direction back to the position in order for them to direct their fire on the German targets. My main job was to be the radio operator for Captain Lewis our B-Battery commanding officer. However, I also worked part time with the forward observation groups that went forward to direct artillery fire for our 105mm howitzers.

We had one year and one month of very hard intensive training at Camp Maxey, Texas. When I look back over our training there, I feel sure that no artillery unit could have had better training to prepare soldiers for what they would be facing in France and Germany than we had in the 250th Field Artillery Battalion.

We left Camp Maxey and traveled by train for Camp Shanks, New Jersey, which was to be our port of embarkation. We arrived at Camp Shanks on February 1, 1944. We boarded our ship and left New York Harbor in the early morning hours of February 11, 1944, and spent a miserable 12½ days crossing the

Atlantic Ocean. We landed in Liverpool, England, on February 23, 1944.

We traveled by train to the town of Atherstone, England, where we trained constantly for the invasion of France to drive the Germans out of France, which they had previously invaded four years earlier. The D-Day invasion started on June 6, 1944, and we left Atherstone on June 8, and moved to Oldham, a suburb of Manchester, England. After serving at Oldham for a short time, we drove to Southampton, England, boarded a ship, crossed the English Channel and landed on Utah Beach with General Patton's 3rd Army.

A few days later, somewhere around St. Lo, we started our 105mm howitzers and moved forward when we could. We passed through the cities of Laval, LeMans, and on to Argentan where we participated in the Argentan-Falaise Gap battle. We fought our way in an eastward direction, bypassed Paris on the south side, and continued to move eastward toward the German border. We were firing many rounds of ammunition as we slowly pushed the Germans back. We eventually reached Strasbourg, France, a large city on the eastern border between France and Germany on Thanksgiving Day, November 23, 1944. From a gun position inside Strasbourg, we fired across the Rhine River into Germany. The 250th was given credit for firing the first round of ammunition across the Rhine River into Germany.

We left Strasbourg and fired many rounds of ammunition as we slowly moved north and west through the French States of Alsace and Lorraine and pulled into gun position about two miles west of Bitche, France, around the 1st of January, 1945. We stayed in this gun position for a month or more through the worst part of the winter. While we were in this gun position, we were given the honor of firing the millionth round of ammunition for the 15th Corp, since we had fired more rounds of ammunition than any other artillery unit in the 15th Corp.

Later we slowly fought our way in a northerly direction and crossed the German border and the Siegfried Line into Germany near Zweibrucken, Germany, on March 21, 1945. Finally, after having fired many, many rounds of ammunition we were on German soil. A couple of days later, we pulled into a gun position near Kleinkarlback, Germany. On the first night in this gun position, I was slightly wounded by a piece of shrapnel from a German artillery shell, for which I received the Purple Heart.

We moved in a northeastward direction, crossed the Rhine River on a pontoon bridge at Worms, Germany, and continued moving eastward toward Nuremburg. From Nuremburg, we slowly fought our way in a southward direction toward Munich, Germany. Shortly after going into gun position on the north edge of Munich, our guns were set up, and we began firing into downtown Munich. I went with a group of volunteers to the town of Dachau to help liberate one of the German SS death camps that units of the 45th Division had found there. We found over 9000 bodies stacked in piles that the SS Troops had killed in the gas chambers during the last few days. Another 2310 bodies were found in 39 boxcars sitting on the railroad sidings there.

After we had crossed the Rhine River, we were moving forward to a new gun position. An intersection ahead of us was crowded with vehicles, so we had to stop for a few minutes. When we stopped, one of our gun trucks in the column behind us had stopped on a small bridge. Just for safety measure, the guys on the truck jumped off to check underneath the bridge to see if any Germans were hiding there. Sure enough, someone was under the bridge. They yelled for him to come out, and a man wearing civilian clothes came crawling out. He was thin and frail. He had been hiding under the bridge to keep the Germans from finding him. He was extremely happy to be liberated by Americans, and he was trying to tell us in Russian language over and over how happy he was.

About that time, the column started moving, and all of us jumped back onto our vehicles. The guys in the truck who had found the Russian motioned for him to climb onto the truck. When we pulled off the road to go into a new position, Captain Lewis began to make arrangement for our new passenger to be placed at a Displaced Persons Camp. His Russian name was long and strange to us. The spelling started out P-e-t-e--- with many more letters. The German word for Russian is "Russkie". We started calling him "Pete, the Russkie". After the guns were set up in our new gun position, Captain Lewis talked with the Russian. He told him that he would send him to a special camp where he could stay until the war was over and then he would be sent back to his home in Russia. He started pleading with Captain Lewis; he did not want to go to camp. He said that he wanted to go with our outfit and fight the Germans. He said that if we would give him a gun that he would fight, fight, fight. Captain Lewis explained and explained to him that we could not have a Russian fighting in the American Army.

"Pete, the Russkie" kept pleading, and finally Captain Lewis called Colonel Jealous, our battalion commander, and explained the problem to him by phone. He told Captain Lewis after their long conversation, to give the Russian an American uniform and let him work with the kitchen truck. His rules: he could wash pots and pans, he could dig holes for the gun trails, and he could dig a trench for a toilet each time that we stopped, but was never to touch a gun. Captain Lewis was told that no one in our unit was to mention to anyone outside of our outfit about the presence of our Russian helper.

Amazingly it worked out. He always had a smile and never complained about the work he was assigned to do—a great asset to B-Battery.

We didn't know it at the time, but when we were firing into Munich, we were firing our last shots of the war. About three days later, we left Munich slowly drove the 100 mile drive to Salzburg, Austria, without firing a shot. On our second day at Salzburg, Captain Lewis called us all together and told us that the war in Europe was over. I will never forget the glorious feeling that I had when he made that announcement. The war was over and I was alive!

Pete stayed with us and worked for a month or maybe two months. He kept telling us he was going to America with the 250th men. An army camp just outside of Salzburg had been converted into Displaced Persons' Camp. I was gone the day he was to leave and go to the DP Camp. However, the other GIs told me that he was extremely disappointed and very distraught and that he sobbed pitifully when he left. I believe that he would have been a good "Pete, the American!" He wanted to come to the United Stated so badly with the 250th.

As far as I am concerned there was not another artillery battalion in World War II that was more efficient than the 250th Field Artillery Battalion. We had so many guys with a great sense of humor that kept us laughing much of the time. However, in combat every man settled down and did his job to the best of his ability. I am very proud to have served with the guys of the 250th Field Artillery Battalion.

Barney Howard at Nice, France—1945

BARNEY HOWARD

I was 20 years old when I got my letter. Congratulation! You have been called for duty to serve your country. The draft age at the time was 20, and my letter came on my birthday—October 26, 1942. I was a farm boy in Greene County, Arkansas. I was a general farm hand on my mother's farm for 4 years prior to army service. We raised cotton, corn, hay and other crops to make ends meet. Our county had to furnish 9 men per month. This was my turn. In early January, 1943, I was on my way to Little Rock. In addition to having to be 20 years old, I had to weigh 120 pounds in order to be drafted. I weighed in at 119. So, they told me to eat a really good meal. About a week later, somewhere around the 12th of January, I was sworn in at Camp Robinson. My first uniform was about a size 46, and I had a 28 waist. Did I ever look funny! When they said "Fall Out" (dismissed from formation) at Camp Robinson, I would go to the chapel. It gave me time to think, but also no one would bother you while you were on chapel grounds. I asked the chaplain to let me pick up cigarette butts. That passed the time while we waited for our next stop. I spent 4 days at Camp Robinson, after which we were put on a train not knowing where we were going. When daylight came the next morning, we saw a sign that said "Welcome to Paris". We laughed and said, "They sent us to France and didn't even give us any training."

When we got to Paris, Texas, and Camp Maxey, there was a huge mess hall. We gathered there for the first pep talk. Colonel Jealous was from Liverpool. He was a good colonel. He never talked mean to anyone that I ever heard. The Colonel told us how good that we would have it. He said that we would have good food, good beds, and leisure time. He said, "You won't have to do anything if you don't want to—but, if you don't; we will make you wish you had." We trained for about a year. Then, we were back on a train and on our way to Camp Shanks, New York. We went out on the town that night—probably got drunk. I remember that we went to the Yacht Club on 52nd Street. The next day we were on the boat and on our way overseas. It was the Dominion Monarch, an English luxury liner. My whole battery slept on the floor in a big theater on board. I remember they had a John Wayne room and other rooms named after movie stars. The Colonel told us that he had bought our tickets for us. He said that he wanted us to know that he bought roundtrip—not one way—because we were all coming back!

I was chosen to drive a truck. I think it was my Lieutenant that said, "Howard, didn't you say that you wanted to drive a truck?" He gave me a test, had me drive forward, backward, etc. He gave me license, and I was a truck driver. My record was good. I only got one ticket. It was in Munich for having three people in the cab. My gunner was Gilbert Suggs. The two of us went to Corpus Christi, Texas, for a couple of weeks to practice shooting flying targets over the Gulf. We did that for hours every day. When we wanted to rest, we would shoot the cable *by accident*. That would give us an hour or so of rest while they fixed the cable. I haven't seen Gilbert since the war. I wonder where he is.

We first landed in Atherstone, England. Atherstone, England, was a small town. We got there in winter time and were there about six months. We did training exercises. Just before D-Day, I hauled German prisoners from Southampton back to Liverpool. We would take German money off the prisoners and put it in a big barrel. We were told that German money was no good. German big bills were no good because it had no backing. The small bills were probably good, but we put it all in a big barrel. I do not know what happened to it after that. I hauled the prisoners about 3 or 4 trips. I would have to go with the prisoners out to the boat where the prisoners would be taken to the United States. One time, I was out at the boat and the boat officer told me that I had to stay with them until the guards came. I waited and waited—thought they were not coming and that I would have to ship out with them. They finally came, and I was relieved.

Around the middle of July, we left Southampton. We boarded a ship. They winched my truck up on board the ship and put it into the cargo hold. The truck was loaded with ammunition. The engine was covered with Cosmoline— petroleum jelly. The boat took us to Normandy beachhead. It took about five days to cross the English Channel. An amphibious boat took me and the truck to within 100 yards of the beach. Water was pouring inside the truck while I was driving. To drive up onto the beach, I put the truck in low gear with all 6 wheels pulling and the gas pedal to the floor. Even at that, the truck was barely moving. Once on land, we searched for route markers. I drove for 5 or 10 miles. Then, we searched for mines. We had to go through with mine clearers because traps were set everywhere. Marbles, diamond rings, and anything valuable was used to entice soldiers to pick them up. Picking it up would activate the mine. When we found a mine, the Lieutenant would take his pistol and shoot it to set off the mine.

We went into battle at St. Lo which was the first city after the Normandy Beachhead. We couldn't go in on D-Day because a place had to be cleared for the 105 Howitzers. Our first shots were fired at St. Lo. We went through St. Lo. The first day, all I saw was burned out tanks—German and American. We saw dead bodies hanging out of tanks, and we just kept on going. Our first night in France, we stayed on a 20 acre farm. We slept on the ground. We each had a shelter half, and two shelter half's would be put together to make a tent.

I remember going through the Falaise Gap where we fought the German 7th Army. This battle took several days. I was told that the German 7th Army was the biggest that Germany had. It was there that I remember seeing a German payroll truck. The pay truck was full of money. When we went through the Gap, there were dead horses for miles. Germans used horses to pull artillery and equipment.

My job in the 250th Field Artillery was to haul artillery ammunition and gas. I drove a GMC 6x6 (six wheels on each side of the truck), that was a 2 and

½ -ton a (deuce and a half) truck. My truck carried 14,000 pounds. We carried 105mm artillery shells. I think shells weighed about 54 pounds apiece. One time, I dropped one of those 105mm artillery shells on my foot! That hurt! It made an injured place on my foot, and I came home from the war with a big lump on my foot where that shell had dropped on it. Years later, my doctor had to remove that lump from the top of my foot so that my shoe would fit. Of course, like everyone else, I didn't take a lot of time off for sick call because we had a war to fight!

On a daily basis—sometimes I made several trips a day—I would drive from our front line artillery battery firing points back to the ammo dump—usually 20 to 30 miles back from the front lines—to pick up a load of ammunition. On my return trip, I would drive ammo up to the gun pits, wherever ammo was needed. As the war progressed, the front lines would get farther away from the ammo dump as the infantry moved forward. The dump didn't move every day. Many nights, we would get loaded at the ammo dump and start our return trip back to our firing points. Bed Check Charlie would get us, and we would have to leave the truck and run into the woods. They dropped shells within a half a block of the truck but never got our truck. Bed Check Charlie, of course, was the name for the German planes that would shoot at us.

I hauled gasoline or ammunition all the time. I would keep the trucks always loaded. If I could not get ammo, I would not unload what I had on the truck. We were supposed to keep the trucks full of ammunition at all times. In fact, there was only one time that we backed up the lines. We backed up about three miles, and it was because we did not have ammunition.

I wore out two trucks during the war. One truck was given to me at Southampton in England. When it got about 30,000 miles on it, they gave me another one. I wore that second truck out too—I wore out two trucks in a year of combat. I drove all over France and into Germany and Austria.

German trucks had the same tires and wheels as our trucks used. Their trucks looked like Fords. Every time we would see a German truck abandoned, I would take my lug wrench and take their tire and wheels. That way, I always carried extras. Sometimes I would have 4 or 5 tires hung onto the side of my truck. We had to be ready for anything. If you ever got into a hole where you would have to spin your wheels, the shrapnel would cut the tire to pieces. I had extras so that I could change my tires and keep going. I had patches and a pump. I would patch the tires myself. I would pump a while, and then Gilbert would pump a while until we could air the tires back up. I had to have two hand grenades in the truck all of the time so that I could destroy the truck if need be. I knew what to do—put one in the cab and one in the truck, pull the pins, and run! I heard that someone once used his hand grenades to kill fish with, but I won't give any names out!

I saw one German and one American ammo dump blown up and burn while I was in the war. I got within a mile and a half of the American ammo dump on my way to reload the truck. A German ME 109 hit the dump and blew it up, 55 gallon barrels went so high in the air that they looked like tin cans up there. I had to sit there all night long. Finally, trailer trucks came into the area, and I loaded up with ammunition from there.

We would drive down the roads in the daytime. We would bypass the Germans because they would be in the woods. At night, Germans trying to get back to their front lines would run over our tents. Often, we would be in a foxhole at night with .50 caliber machine gun shooting over our head. Believe me, you stayed in that foxhole. One night, I stopped my truck loaded with ammo. When I woke up the next morning, I saw a leg with a new boot on it hanging from a tree. The leg had been blown into the tree from an explosion.

When we stopped at night, we had 2 hours shifts of guard duty. One man would stay awake, and one would sleep. You stayed in the foxhole or tent all night because if you were out in the night, the risk was that a guard would shoot you. One night, the Germans came in on us. It was Gilbert's watch. I got up when I heard Gilbert shoot. We didn't know that he shot him, but with daylight we found a German that he had hit. We found 4 more Germans alive in the woods. We flushed them out. We had to shoot one that would not stop. We captured the other three. This was in France somewhere. My buddy (I can't remember his name) was a cracker jack shot. He gave me good advice. He told me to always keep my rifle clean, and I listened to him. I became quite a good shot, and it later helped me when I started duck hunting with my son-in-law!

We didn't have time to think about being scared. We had to just keep going, watch our backs, and watch out for each other. When we were sick, we just kept going. I didn't ever want to go on sick call. We had work to do and no time to waste. If you were put on sick call, your unit would not wait on you. They had to move on and you could be left behind. If that happened, you might be assigned to another unit who was short a man. I always wanted to stay with my friends and the guys that I knew and trusted.

In the dark, you could see strange things. Everything seemed to move in the dark! One night we parked by an apple tree. The next morning Gilbert asked me if "that tree walked with me last night." I saw lots of walking trees over there. That's when you are really scared.

Somewhere in France, we were fixing a flat in a mud hole at night. One guy kept turning on a flashlight to see. We kept telling him to turn it off, but he would turn it back on just to see for a second. Finally, someone said, "Let him go. They will turn it out for him in a minute." They meant that if that guy kept shining that light, a German soldier or a German airplane would see the light and shoot him.

We passed the 999th Field Artillery. They would load and fire out there about 20 miles away. They fired Long Toms (155 field range artillery rifles). They would write this on the projectile, "Here's a Christmas present for you, Mr. Hitler."

An L-5 or L-3 aerial observer plane hit the ground one time. There were two trees down there. He had to go between them. The crash took both wings off. I hauled the plane back for repairs. After that, we nicknamed him "Pilot."

We had an idea that things were changing. One time, I remember these German planes came into our area. One of them hung a white bed sheet size piece of fabric out of the plane. They were allowed to land and surrender.

When we hit the autobahn in Munich, we went straight to Salzburg, Austria. When we got there, we drove our trucks into a field and parked bumper to bumper. This was our first clue that something was up. We usually drove at 100-300 yard intervals between trucks. When the convoy stopped, we got out of our trucks. We were all congregated together in formation, and we were told to stack our rifles. We knew the war was over when we drove into that big area, and drove close together in convoy. That was the last time that I saw my rifle. I carried that rifle through two trucks and a war. I wonder what happened to it. I wish that I had it now to give it to my son-in-law.

After the war in Germany ended, I was still driving a GMC truck in Salzburg, Austria. We were with the 975th Field Artillery for my last month in the army. They drove Diamond T's 6x6, 2 and a half ton trucks that pulled their howitzers. We weren't told anything about where we were going. We thought that we were "fixing to go to Japan." Instead, after V-J Day, we came from Salzburg back to the states.

We drove down to the Riviera on furlough. This was after the war. It was beautiful there. Driving through the Alps, I burned out the brakes on my truck. They even caught on fire. By the time we got through the Alps, I was stopping that truck with only the gears. I was on a work detail driving a load of our soldiers down there for a furlough. We got to Nice, France, and I turned in the truck to this big truck yard. They gave me a card to use when I came back to retrieve it. We stayed in the Hotel Continental—everything free for about seven days. When we went back for the truck, the brakes had been repaired. I drove us back to Salzburg.

We came home on a Liberty Ship. That was a rough ride—beats you to death. I was sea sick both ways anyway. Coming home, a storm came up. After the storm, we didn't have any life emergency boats. They capsized and floated away during the storm.

The war was over. We all came home and went our separate ways. We depended on each other for our lives. Brothers we were and brother we are. Those three years were quite a tussle. I wouldn't trade it. I would do it again. I made it through it. We had a job to do, and we did it well!

Since 1945, my home has been in Paragould, Arkansas, not far from where I was born. I met and married my wife, Bernice Howard—she kept her last name because she was a Howard too! We have a daughter, Shelia and son-in-law, Dennis. After the war, I farmed; worked in California fruit orchards; worked in a gas station; drove a delivery grocery truck; and then I went into my own business as a used car salesman. I have had a good life since the war! We all had to fight to save our country, and I am glad for what we did.

Jada M. McGuire—1943

Jada M. McGuire

ARTILLERY A-BATTERY: CLERK

I was 18 when I was inducted at Camp Robinson in January 14, 1943. Two days later I arrived at Camp Maxey for my basic training. After being greeted at Camp Maxey by the coldest wind that Texas was capable of offering and by five of the toughest first sergeants ever assembled in one unit, these rookies settled down to the job of learning what a 105mm howitzer was supposed to do and could do. They had come from many states but mainly from Arkansas, Louisiana, Oklahoma, New York and Texas.

Records reveal that the 250th Field Artillery Battalion was activated September 25, 1942, at Camp Maxey, Paris, Texas, and deactivated March 8, 1946, at Camp Kilmer, New Jersey. What happened in between was the compilation of a record so amazing and colorful that probably no other artillery battalion has before or since come close to it.

Commanded by Lt. Col. William K. Jealous of Fair Lawn, New Jersey, from its inception, the 250th brought from Fort Sill, Oklahoma, a full complement of officers, a large part of whom were fresh out of OCS, and a hard-hearted group of non-coms, both Regular Army type and civilian soldiers. These officers and non-coms fashioned a fighting unit, somehow, from about 500 of the rawest, grumblingest but proudest recruits that Paris, Texas, has ever had.

In the summer of 1943, following half a year of intensive training, the 250th with its five batteries: Headquarters, A, B, C, and Service Battery–plus its attached medical unit, went on a pleasure trip to the pine tree, sand bur, tick-ridden part of Louisiana near Fort Polk. Here we were privileged to be a part of six weeks of maneuvers under simulated combat conditions. It might be pointed out that several of the battalions' members would party a bit overtime in Leesville one weekend and lost their stripes.

Back to the comfortable barracks at Camp Maxey after living in the poison oak for what seemed like an eternity, the 250th settled down to several more months of rigid training. By now rumors were making the rounds. The possibility of combat seemed imminent. Would it be Europe or the South Pacific?

A two-day train trip in late January, 1944, brought the 250th to Camp Shanks, New York, and the unit set sail for England February 11 aboard the luxury liner, HMS Dominion Monarch. A steady diet of baked fish and baked potatoes twice a day for 13 days added to the enjoyment of this cruise across the bouncy waters of the Atlantic.

Landing at Liverpool February 23, we went directly to the thriving metropolis of Atherstone in Warwickshire. It is still a mystery how so many pubs could operate at a profit in Atherstone. We ate fish 'n chips and continued combat training for about four months. Then they made MP's out of us and we guarded prisoners of war in Northern England until time to go across the Channel with General Patton's Third Army.

Southampton was the point of departure from England, and while waiting on the English Channel aboard ship for about five days, the 250th found out what war sounded like. We landed in Normandy July 24, 1944, in time to be a part of the St. Lo breakthrough with the XV Corps. After being loaned to the 79th Division for a brief period, we became a part of the famed Second French Armored Division, commanded by General LeClerc. That's where the fun started. The Second Armored, with our support, fought through LeMans, Alencon, Louvigny, Mortree and Argentan. The 250th was deeply involved in the complete destruction of the German Seventh Army in the Argentan-Falaise Gap.

Following a 101 mile march due east, the 250th and other units exhausted their gas and oil supply and bivouacked about 30 miles outside Paris. Our French friends had gone into Paris to receive a wild and warm welcome. After two weeks of partying in the French Capital, the Second Armored decided it was time to get back into the thick of things. So, on September 11, the Second Armored took off again with the 250th right behind. Names like Vittel, Dompaine, Epinal and Rambervillers became common conversation in those days and the 250th was given many important targets and fired hundreds of effective rounds. Then there came a taste of defensive fighting when the 250th helped protect XV Corps' right flank while the 79th Division routed the enemy from the Forrest of Parroy.

On November 21 the 250th started crossing the dangerous Vosges Mountains with the Second Armored leading the way. This was the beginning of the drive to Strasbourg which won acclaim for the battalion from General LeClerc's Division. Crossing of the Vosges was highlighted by a night of misery when our vehicles were caught by darkness, bumper to bumper on a narrow road in the dense, wooded mountains. On November 23, Thanksgiving Day, the 250th, supporting advance units of the Second French Armored, rushed into Strasbourg with such speed that the enemy was completely surprised and the city's natives gratefully acclaimed the arrival of American troops.

Here's what *Stars and Stripes* had to say about the Strasbourg venture quoting Lt. William V. Loncaric of the 250th who furnished the information: INTO STRASBOURG—in compliance to your request as to when Strasbourg officially fell, I shall endeavor to give you the correct version. The reconnaissance party of our Artillery Battalion preceded by several tanks of the 2nd Armored Division (French: 2e Division Blindée, 2e DB) entered the city limits of Strasbourg at 1145, November 23. The batteries took position in the city and began their interdictory fires on crossroads west of Kehl at 1400. Snipers were very active until noon the following day. Our unit also boasts as the first American unit to fire across the Rhine into Germany. The Krauts didn't have the privilege of enjoying Thanksgiving in Strasbourg."

For this action the French awarded the 250th a brigade citation. Also the battalion received the Distinguished Unit Citation Streamer embroidered *Saverne Gap.*

The 250th joined the 100th Division December 6 and attacked the Maginot lines as far as Bitche. We were getting ready to push on with this attack when the Germans counter-attacked on December 31 and January 1. Counter battery and screaming 88s became everyday things to men of the 250th. The Ardennes break-through by the enemy had happened a few days before and XV Corps did not have enough forces to continue the offensive. As a result we went into "winter quarters" in a defensive position for 10 weeks around the Rohrback, Montbrunn, Enchenberg, Petit Rederching and Lemberg area.

The Stars and Stripes ran the following item February 9, 1945: "Jolt for Jerry— with VX Corps, France – Artillery of this corps has hurled its millionth round against the enemy. A 105mm howitzer of the 250th Field Artillery Battalion fired the autographed shell and scored a hit on a German strong point.

On March 15, XV Corps attacked and we were in the thick of battle again. With the 100th Division we moved into Bitche, then to Liederschied. There we left the 100th and became attached to the 3rd Infantry Division. Part of the assignment with the 3rd was assaulting the Siegfried Line. The unit moved rapidly through such places as Zweibrucken, Auerbach, Steinalben, Trippstadt, Frankenstein, Bad Durkheim and many others. We crossed the Rhine River at Worms on a pontoon bridge the night of March 26. Then on March 31 the 250th crossed another river-the main-at Worth. During the next few days the 250th was relieved from the 3rd Division and attached to the 45th Division. Later on the battalion fired a number of concentrations for the 106th Cavalry Group. Throughout all this rapid movement near Bamberg and Nurnberg, the 250th was in constant threat of attack by an SS Division just five or six kilometer to the Southeast.

From April 19 up to early May the 250th was attached to various units and moved on through places such as Schrobenhausen, Gerolsbach, Pertershausen, Hohenkammer and Unter Schleisheim. In this latter position near Munich, firing for the 20th Armored Division, the 250th Field Artillery Battalion fired its last rounds of the war in Europe. Moving on through Munich and down to Glanegg, Austria, just south of Salzburg, the battalion went into bivouac on the north edge of the Alps. It was here that word was received on May 8, 1945, of the victory in Europe. A well-deserved victory celebration lasted well into the night.

The next few months saw members of the 250th leave for other units in preparation for the trip to assembly areas on the coast of France and onto that long-awaited mustering out event. Salzburg, the home of Mozart, furnished a comfortable life for the short time the men of the 250th were there. Most battalion members were allowed to visit other parts of Europe as a token payment for the many months of hard combat life that had been endured.

At this point it is appropriate to quote liberally from a history of the 250th Field Artillery Battalion as written and addressed to the officers and men of the unit by its commander, Lt. Col. William K. Jealous on June 25, 1945. Much of the above records and events also came from Colonel Jealous' history. I quote:

"The European War having been brought to a successful close I wish to thank every member of the 250th Field Artillery Battalion for the enthusiasm, esprit de corps, and cooperation you displayed throughout your fight across France and Germany. I also commend you for performing your duties in such an efficient manner that every unit with which the 250th Field Artillery Battalion fought spared no words of praise for you.

Yours was not an easy job. As a separate light Field Artillery Battalion in XV Corps, you were constantly being moved, attached first to one unit then another, but always where the fighting was hottest. You have worked with Infantry Divisions, Armored Divisions, an Engineer Battalion, a Calvary Group and to quote the words of the Commanding General XV Corps Artillery, Brig. General Edward S. Ott, "Not once did you request relief or complain of your assignment." In addition to the verbal commendations from many units, you received a brigade citation from the 2nd French Armored Division, a letter of commendation from the 100th Infantry Division, U.S. Army, and a letter of congratulations from Commanding General, XV Corps Artillery. The 2nd French Armored Division presented 20 Croix de Guerre medals to members of the battalion and over 100 received the Bronze Star Medal. All members of the battalion earned five battle stars, one each for the campaigns of Normandy, Northern France, Rhineland and Central Europe and Ardennes-Alsace.

In your fighting from the pubs in England to the poop (conformation) sheets in Austria you have had the opportunity to visit several countries and to observe the people of these countries. I trust that all of you will take home an understanding of these peoples and the complexity of their problem of living together on the continent of Europe. The future attitude of our United States towards Europe will be determined to a great extent by you returning veterans.

The Splendid record set by the 250th Field Artillery Battalion could not have been accomplished without the faithful performance by each man of his own particular job whether it be cook, cannoneer (artillery gunner), clerk or wireman. I join you in saying that I am proud to have been a member of the 250th 'Automatic' Artillery Battalion."

Wm. K. Jealous,
Lt. Col. FA, Commanding

I returned home on December 7, 1945. It was one month short of being three years with a Corporal rank.

Jada McGuire—2005

Roger Livermore: Paris, France—1945

Roger Livermore

I was just 18 when I was inducted into the Army in May of 1943. I was sent to Ft. Devens, MA and then to Camp Picket, VA for my basic training. Camp Picket was in the middle of nowhere. From Camp Picket I transferred to Ft. Benjamin Harrison General Hospital in Indianapolis, Indiana. I left from Indiana to Camp Reynolds, PA, which was another hellhole. I didn't like it—it was cold and rainy. We were in the northwest part. While there, I received rifle training and qualified as a marksman even though I was still a medic. We had to take a rifle apart and put it back together blindfolded so if in the dark out we would know what to do.

Next, I was bound for New York for embarkation, but was taken out and put in the hospital for a minor operation. That was when I joined the 250th Battalion as a replacement. We shipped out from the New York Harbor on the Dominion Monarch. I remember it took about two weeks for the crossing. We were in a convoy with other ships; there were still German subs in the Atlantic. We landed in Liverpool, England and taken to Camp Merevale at Atherstone, Warwick, England. Some of us were taken to the estate of Warwick Castle. While in Warwickshire, England on the grounds of Warwick Castle we were told not to bother the lord because he was nice enough to let us use the grounds. While in England I visited

Stratford on Avon, the birthplace of Shakespeare, Sherwood Forest and the flattened town of Coventry. We did not have any air raids as we were not near any industrial targets. I did hear the German planes going over to bomb Birmingham.

The equipment had been waterproofed for the invasion, but at the last minute we were pulled out and sent to the border of Scotland and England to take charge of a POW Camp for German prisoners captured in the invasion. The 250th left for France in July of 1944 and I spent my 20th Birthday on the boat in the English Channel waiting for room to be taken to shore. I celebrated by eating a C-ration when we were supposed to eat only K-ration. The K-rations were not too good.

I remember we were with General Patton when we had to stay in position for a week because the supplies were not keeping up with us. There is remembrance of our being assigned to the 2nd French Armored Division as they were made up mostly of Moroccans with the red "fezes" hat.

While in France we slept on the ground most of the time. We dug foxholes in case of enemy attack. In some positions the foxholes filled with water as soon as they were dug. I remember one scare where a fellow jumped in the filled up foxhole. It was a false alarm and everybody had a good laugh afterwards when he came up dripping water. I put empty shell casings in the bottom of mine and dug a drain to prevent the water from coming in.

My tent partner took ill and I sent him to a hospital with appendicitis. He never returned so I had his rifle during the rest of the war even though I was a medic and was not suppose to carry a gun. While riding on top of a 6x6 at night through the French towns I would have returned fire if fired upon.

There were orders to keep blackouts. Men would go into town and light a bonfire and dare the Germans to do anything about it. During the war of the "Bulge" I was in Strasbourg. We were strung out so thin that the Germans could have walked through our positions anytime. I vaguely remember when some the battalion was hit by German aircraft in the Bitche area, and the bridge across the Rhine. The battalion was southeast of the Bulge. I don't think I would be here today if I had been there.

When the war ended in Munich close to where the Dachau concentration

Camp was located and liberated. I get so mad now when I hear some young people say that this never happened. I was there and saw it so I know it indeed did happen.

I was transferred outside of Salzburg, Austria for training to go to the South Pacific which never happened. Many of the 250th had points to go home but as I was a replacement I did not. I was changed from medic to job of company clerk, which was my position when I came home. They were retraining on an 8 inch gun which was a change from the 105s.

While in Austria after the war we took several trips; a couple of weekends in Paris and to Brussels, a week on a Lake in Austria, and a week or so to the French Riviera after crossing the French Alps by truck. I went skiing in the Austrian Alps on Labor Day weekend. I also saw Hitler's Retreat in the Alps.

I had been transferred to 26th Yankee Division for discharge. We had a horrible trip back as we hit a storm after leaving the Gibraltar and I was seasick for seven days. The trip was so rough. I would have died if my buddies had not brought me apples and crackers from mess hall, which is the only thing I could eat.

The Dominion Monarch that we went overseas on was a nice ship compared to the ships we came home on. There were two; the Liberty and the Victory. I do not remember which one I came home on, but I do know it was the bigger of the two. We passed smaller ones on our way home.

Another buddy and I played cribbage on the way back while everyone else played poker or craps. When we landed in Norfolk, VA the money was in the hands of a few people. We had been given our pay before leaving Marseilles.

I landed at Norfolk and immediately noticed the difference between Germany and the U. S. In Germany, you saw a nice house with no cars and in the U.S. you saw two nice cars with a rundown house. Finally, in the Norfolk area we took a train back to Ft. Devens where I was discharged at the beginning of January 1946.

My medic training came in useful several times in civilian life. I went to Boston University on the GI bill and got my degree. I am now retired, but "meals on wheels" and sell real estate when I feel like it.

Kenneth Turner

Kenneth Turner

B-BATTERY: ARTILLERY-GUNNER

I entered the Army December of 1942. I spent one night at Camp Robinson in Little Rock, Arkansas and then was sent to Camp Maxey, Paris Texas, for my basic training. We were sent to Louisiana for six weeks of maneuvers near Fort Polk and then, it was back to Camp Maxey to start preparation for overseas duty.

We left on a train for Camp Shanks, New York. We left the New York Harbor on the Dominion Monarch and landed in Liverpool, England on February 23, 1944. I had my 21st birthday while on ship at Liverpool.

We departed Southampton, England and arrived on the Normandy coast on July 23, 1944. We waited a few days on ship; the English Channel was too rough making it unsafe to unload.

Our battalion spent a lot of time with General LeClerc's 2nd French Armored Division, but we never got to go in to liberate Paris with them, but had to wait on the outskirts. We were with General LeClerc when we went into Strasbourg. We captured 2600 prisoners that we left in other hands. General Eisenhower had decided to abandon Strasbourg that was again at risk. General Charles de Gaulle sent a warning if the Allied vacated Strasbourg that he would remove his troops from the Allied command. Allied troops were left to protect Strasbourg.

We set for thirteen weeks in the snow at Bitche area; had to white wash everything to blend in with the snow. It was an area of the Maginot lines and pillboxes. The one thing I remember—there was much hurry up and wait.

We crossed the Rhine at Worms and continued working our way to Dachau and then on to Munich. Munich was where the 250th saw their last battle. The battalion moved on down to Salzburg, Austria. Our battery was billeted in the village of Obermoos.

We were sent home by points. I didn't have enough so I volunteered with 155th Field Artillery. The war ended in Japan so we weren't needed over there.

I shipped out for home from LeHarve, France on the LST; strait of Gibraltar to the Atlantic and docked in Boston. It was then on to St. Louis, Missouri to Jefferson Barracks. I left Missouri on a troop train to little Rock Arkansas. I was only 40 miles from home so I hitch hiked, for I would have had to wait until 10:00 the next morning for a train. There were no buses going my direction. I got home on Thanksgiving Day 1945. I got to see my son that was born six months after I was drafted.

I had two brothers in service: one was in Italy and the other was in Africa. We were just young men that never knew how much danger we were really in—perhaps that was a good thing!

Kenneth Turner (photo center)

Monte Bankhead (top)

Monte Bankhead, (bottom), standing beside Capt. Howard H. Leslie "A" Battery Commander's car. Monte mostly rode in a jeep, but did ride in the CC as a passenger at times.

Monte Bankhead

ARTILLERY A-BATTERY: FORWARD OBSERVER

I entered the army on December 19, 1942. I had my basic training at Camp Maxey, Paris, Texas. I was assigned to the 250th Field Artillery Battalion and worked with the Motor Officer and Forward Observation Advance Party Team, 1st Lt. Longwell, and 1st Lt. John F. Roberts A-Battery Executive. Captain Howard H. Leslie was A-Battery Commander.

The 250th Field Artillery was organized as a non-divisional 105 mm Howitzer Battalion. It was commanded by Lt. Col. William K. Jealous. As a separate battalion, it experienced many demanding situations and operations far more than standard divisional units. And with much training, was able to augment divisional artillery.

After many days of training at Camp Maxey, Texas, we were put on alert and left for Camp Shanks, New York—then on to England on a British ship. We had British civilians on the ship, so we were served twice a day—a diet of baked and fried fish for two weeks. Rough seas and the menu didn't go well together.

This troop convoy proved to be the largest of the war—escorted by aircraft carriers and every known combat vessel.

After two weeks, we arrived at Liverpool, England. In England, we received more training, such as firing in Wales. It was in Wales where General George

C. Patton inspected us. Maybe it was because the 250th Battalion scored high in firing exams that he chose us to be part of his 3rd Army and informed us we would be charter members.

We crossed the English Channel and landed at Normandy (Utah) Beach. The sight was beyond description—sunken vessels, equipment everywhere, troops and equipment were unloaded through a drawbridge at the front of the ship.

The Corps Artillery that we were most frequently a part of General Wade Haislip XV Corps and the division to which we were most regularly assigned was the 2nd French Armored Division, commanded by General LeClerc.

General LeClerc was captured at Dunkirk, France, and taken as a prisoner by the Germans. He took an oath to return and recapture Paris and Strasbourg. He escaped, worked his way to South Africa and with help he set up a new division with professional Moroccan soldiers. He fought his way through the sand of the African desert to the north shores of Africa, then over to England to become part of the 3rd Army.

Our advances in France were slow—fighting the Hedgerow battles and all the elements. Next we took Fougers, Dompaire, Laval and Argentine-Falaise Gap.

It was at the Argentine-Gap where we had a major role in the closing of the Gap and the annihilation of the German 7th Army commanded by General Rommel. The battalion fired 2,074 rounds from Alemenches into the Falaise Gap.

The forward observer had the job of setting up forward observation post looking for targets and reporting back to their assigned position. The observers' report back would affect whether the target was destroyed or whether there was a need for more firing. Gunners would be given a certain location, direction, elevation and the exact time to fire. Forward Observers were rotated up front every 3 days—24 hours a day, then a fresh group would replace us for three days.

We also were involved in the later part of the breakthrough at St. Lo. (The battle of St. Lo was one of the great epics of WWII.) For every foot of advance there was a casualty.

The battalion was part of the French 2nd Armored Division when Paris was liberated. It was decided not to destroy Paris. Gen. LeClerc requested that Gen. Patton allow him to go into Paris first, this was a political matter. Gen.

Eisenhower made the final decision. The 250th never went into Paris, but stayed outside. It was then that the battalion ran out of gas and had to set and wait a week for a supply.

The Vosges Mountains was almost impossible for the allied to cross. Neither side had attempted to cross these mountains during WWI. No army in modern history attempted it. It was the opinion that due to the nature of these mountains, they would be forced to go through the gap, in order to reach the Alsace-Lorraine Valley on the other side. The Vosges Gap is a valley some 30 or 40 miles in width. The Vosges Mountains extend northward into France from Switzerland, and forms a barrier between the rest of France and the Alsace-Lorraine Valley. Some of the fiercest trench fighting of WWI was in the Gap.

The French 2nd Armored were able to plug into German telephone lines and one of the officers who spoke German, warned the Germans that a huge allied force was approaching the Gap and to immediately rush as many troops as possible there.

This apparently worked, because with the 2nd French Armored Division we were able to go up and over the Alsace-Lorraine Valley, then on into Strasbourg on Thanksgiving Day—two days ahead of any American troops. The Germans were completely unaware of our presence. We were the first Americans to fire across the Rhine River from Strasbourg.

It was getting colder and winter was just around the corner. The Battle of the Bulge was beginning to take place. At this time we were in what was called the "Colmar Pocket". We were assigned to a holding position protecting the south flanks.

The stars and Stripes published the following item Feb. 9, 1945, "Jolt and Jerry", where the XV Corps Artillery hurled the millionth round against the enemy. A 105mm howitzer of the 250th FA Bn fired the autographed shell, and the gun crew was comprised of Generals and Colonels.

Captain Leslie was slightly wounded in action on November 17, 1944 by shrapnel near Montigny, France. Lt. Roberts was A-Battery Commander during Captain Leslie's absence. Captain Leslie returned to duty the first part of February in 1945.

I rode mostly in the jeep with the forward observers, but did ride in the "CC" Commander's car. When I rode in the Commander's car it was as a passenger. I remember the Commander's car had side curtains.

After crossing the Danube River on Pontoon bridges we heard President Roosevelt had died. We then arrived at Nuremburg where a lot of fighting took place. Next, we arrived at Dachau Concentration Camp, 10 miles northwest of Munich. The horrible sight we saw will never be forgotten. We saw railroad cars loaded with bodies waiting to be cremated. The soldiers just all went berserk, hunting down all S.S. troops they could find. I took a picture looking down in one of the boxcars. I have an enlargement of it.

And some people have the nerve to say there was no Holocaust. Berchtesgaden was to be the last Nazi stronghold (10 miles south of Salzberg, Austria). This is where the "Eagle Nest" was located. Hitler had this built. Located high up in the Bavarian Alps, where one could see for miles and miles.

Then it was on to Munich where an ultimatum to surrender was given but refused by the S.S. The total destruction of Munich began.

The 250th completed 297 consecutive days in combat without relief.

I was sent home October 20, 1945 with a T/4 rank. I came home on a Liberty ship into New York … back home after 2 years and 10 months.

Monte received two personal awards: By direction of the President was awarded the Bronze Star Medal for his heroic achievement in action on January 1, 1945, in the vicinity of Rimling, France. Despite heavy enemy fire on his forward observation station, Monte, radio operator, remained at his post calmly transmitting fire orders. When the hostile shelling increased and it became necessary to move the outpost to an alternate position he ably assisted the forward observer in accomplishing this with a minimum of delay, and then, despite the continuing enemy action, resumed his duties to permit delivery at accurate and destructive artillery fire on hostile targets and Citation for Meritorious Military Duty along with the *several* awards the 250th Battalion received. Monte was among those honored as a World War II Memorial dedicated in Washington, D.C, in 2004.

Monte made a complete detailed scrapbook of his war experience. He remains close with other members, attending an annual reunion and keeping in touch through newsletters. The Battalion was 537 strong at one time. "We are close knit," he said. "Just like a big family."

L–R: Wayne Ward, Joe Festervan and Allen Bandy

ALLEN BANDY

I was inducted at Little Rock, AR at Camp Robinson. From Camp Robinson I was sent to Camp Maxey, Paris, Texas for my basic training. Later, the battalion was sent to Louisiana maneuvers before loading up for overseas duty.

I drove a truck that pulled the 105mm howitzer. I had fun! I didn't care whether the sun came up or down as long as I had something to drink. I would keep something to drink under the seat and if the officers wanted something to drink they knew where to come!

For me—trouble wasn't hard to find; it just seem to be there! When we got in artillery position there wasn't much for me to do but stand around. I would sometimes go on foot in search of a house where I would get rabbit or chicken to bring back to the other men for something to eat. At other times I'd camouflage the truck and go looking for something to get soused with.

While in Munich Joe Festervan and I were looking for something to drink. Joe wasn't much of a drinker, but he went with me. While we were looking we came upon this airfield where there was this ME109 (Messerschmitt) single-seated German fighter. There was a pilot sitting in it and had it running, but he jump out and took off. Those 109s sounded just like a bumble bee and from a distance would look like a little speck in the sky. They came over strafing. The

Germans used the Autobahn for an airstrip. They would keep their airplane off in the woods. The media had a painted green strip that was used for airplanes to land and take off.

There were grenades lying around and I would pick them up and put them in the truck. Using the German grenades, I would stop at the river and kill and clean some fish to eat. We would use our mess kit to fry them.

After VE-Day the 250th Battalion was split up and I was sent to the 975th Artillery Battalion with the 101st Infantry—New York, National Guard outfit. I was transferred from "B" to the "C" Battery. Major Fuller saw that I didn't have to go to the South Pacific. He said we had fought one war and that was enough.

We were shuffled around on the coast around Le Harve, France. When I received orders that I could go home I was to be shipped out from Camp Lucky Strike. Camp Lucky Strike was where they had one of the big World War I battles. There were ships coming in and going out. We had to wait around for a ship, for they were moving soldiers from the South Pacific home at the same time. Some of us got tired of waiting and started turning things up-side-down. They wanted rid of us—we left on a little Liberty ship that was built primarily for freight, so speed was not a priority. We got into a rough storm coming home. On ship we were bounced around; it made you think you'd not make it home. I thought the ship's bottom would come out. There were many soldiers on Liberty ships coming home that Christmas day in 1945.

We docked in Virginia and I took a train from there to Shelby, Mississippi. Mother didn't know I was coming home—I had not written for 6 months. My mother had moved and I didn't know where. I ask the taxi driver if he knew and he said he did. I said, "Take me there." When I knocked on the door my sister answered and she just stood there for a few seconds—kind of in shock. My Mother said, "Who is it?" Finally, my sister said, "It is Allen." My Mother came to the door and grabbed me with my duffle bags and all in hand. I returned home to later quit drinking after I got married.

The 250th Battalion would be the first Allied unit to shoot across the Rhine River into Germany. T. O. Johnson's gun of our B-Battery was used to shot the 1,000,000th round of ammunition into Bitche, France. Each artillery fire was recorded.

I would do anything for a laugh, but I don't think I could go through another war like that!

Lindel McCullough

LINDEL McCULLOUGH

ARTILLERY C-BATTERY: WIRE "TELEPHONE" SECTION & BARBER

I was inducted in December 1942 at Little Rock, Arkansas and sent to Paris, Texas to Camp Maxey for my basic training. I had worked for the CCC (Civil Conservation Corps) for two years before I entered the army. I was made corporal right away and assigned to wire section. While at Camp Maxey there was a barbershop where you could get a haircut anytime, but when we were sent to the fields in Louisiana for maneuvers orders were: not to go into town for 8 weeks. I took my clipper set with me. One Saturday to another fella I said, "Come over here and let me cut your hair." He responded, "I am not going to let you cut my hair!" Well, by the time I was about through with his hair others started to line up for a haircut. When Captain Glazer went to headquarters old Colonel Jealous said, "I thought I told you NO going into town for eight weeks!" He thought with the men sporting a fresh haircut that they had gone into town.

One day Major Fuller came to get his haircut. He asked if I wanted to cut hair and I told him I had guard duty and such. He said, "I'll take care of that!" That I would have no guard duty, or extra detail work of any kind, no formation, but I did go out for roll call.

After maneuvers we returned to Camp Maxey where they were getting us ready to ship us overseas. We left Paris, Texas in February of 1944 by train for a two day trip into New York. We left the New York Port for Europe crossing the Atlantic, in a large convoy on the night of February 11, 1944. While on the Dominion Monarch we experienced 12 and half days of rough seas taking the northern route. We arrived at Liverpool, England on February 23rd. We were based in and around Atherstone until we went to Normandy. The battalion shipped out of Southampton on July 18, 1944, and arrived on the coast of Normandy, France next morning. The 250th didn't go to shore until the 25th. The English Channel was too rough making it unsafe to disembark from the U.S.S. Herkimer to move troops on shore. Once ashore the battalion was introduced to our first combat introduction. We had little sleep that night—a lasting memory of several gas warning alerts! We could hear gun and our tanks firing in the distance.

At night, German aircraft always were searching for us. They would try to strafe us. We always had our lights out. We had been told: *Do not shoot at Bed Check Charlie!*

The battalion had been assigned to General Patton who would come in from England on July 31st. Once there, Patton would moved swiftly across France— our second introduction to war. Patton was ardent to keep his army moving. We would transfer from General Patton to General Patch's 7th Army around Lunéville on September 28, 1944.

While in Germany Wilbur Johnson and I were together when I spied a big, white hog rooting on the bank across the river. Well, I decided I would like to get that hog. I told Captain Glazer and he said, "If you are going to get it, you'd had better hurry for we are going to move out." I don't remember the name of the river, but it was big—not like the Rhine River. It was on the east side of the river where the Germans were and we were on the west side. The bank was pretty high so it would have been hard for them to see us. Wilbur and I made out hurriedly for the other side for our kill. I rowed while *good ole* Wilbur was bailer dipping. I shot the hog, and when we were putting it in the boat, it just about tipped the boat over. The river was deep.

We were bivouac where there was a saw mill. We used shavings from molded wood that had been molded out to build a fire. We got the water real hot using a barrel of water that had been setting there and used a rope to heist the hog down in the hot water. We scraped the scald hog the best we could. Our Mess Sergeant Palmer of "C" Battery kitchen wasn't too happy with my kill. He said, "It is not U.S. inspected!" Captain Glazer said, "I'll take care of that!" He took a piece of chalk and marked U.S. #1 prime. Sgt. Palmer didn't fix all of it for he wasn't happy about it not being U.S. inspected. We did get our hog feast.

After the war was over and while at Austria, I said to Norwood Malone from New Orleans, let's go to Hitler's retreat "Eagles Nest". We weren't supposed to go up there. While in route there we passed a captain and some men walking. We were in a truck—the first to arrive at Berchtesgaden. We got a few things and went down to the cellar; a big building that had wine and champagne dated back to 1863. We started to load the truck and the captain came up and told us to put it back. We put back two cases and while the captain was downstairs Malone wanted to shoot the captain. He said, "Nobody would hear it down here." I told him not to for it would get him into serious trouble. I came on up out of the cellar ahead of Malone. When he came on up from the cellar—I never heard any shots. While the captain was down in the cellar, we ran to the truck and drove off. We got 14 cases of champagne and 16 cases of wine.

While in Louisiana on maneuvers our Sergeant got sick and went to the Doctor. The Doctor wasn't the best of doctors. He told our Sergeant he had an ulcer and he was going to send him home. Sergeant told me he wasn't sick but he wasn't going to tell anyone else. Captain Glazer was next in line and he came to me and told me he was going to make me Sergeant and would send papers to the 250th Headquarters. Then, while in formation, Capt. Glazer announced: that from now on, McCullough is to be addressed as "Sergeant".

I had an Uncle to pass away and was going home for a few days. Glazer told me to get my stripes and sew them on before I left. Upon my return trip from home, Capt. Glazer came to me and told me the Sergeant orders were turned down, that there were men coming in from the Air Section. One of them was made sergeant with no experience in wire section. We got tired of not having orders given to us and one day we just sat in the truck. Captain Glazer came up not so happy and asked, "why haven't you got the wire in?" I told him they put someone in charge unable to give order detail. Glazer said, "You know how; get out and do it!" We had two trucks; one went one way, and one went the other way. Back at the barracks Captain Glazer got onto both of us. The new Sergeant suggested that I take over his job, but Glazer said, "I can't do that—you earned it!" So it was worked out that while in the field that I would act as Sergeant. Field sergeant I was for two years, but never legal!

I made more money as barber than I would have as sergeant. I made 50 cents a head, which was pretty good money. I barbered for two years.

After the war the 250th was split up into and I was sent the 975th Battalion. Lt. Levenson was transferred to "C" battery to wire-section while the battalion was in France in November. He was overseeing a Displaced Polish Camp and came to me and asked if I would assist him and bring my crew. There were 13,433 Polish.

Lt. Levenson got an opportunity to go on a furlough to Switzerland by way around France when he got sick and had to be hospitalized. He never returned and I was left in charge of the Polish Camp.

The United Nations sent two men from the United States and one from London, England. One day I happen to meet the three when they got off the train in Austria. They were asking for directions to a hotel in Moniholz, Austria and the people responded (ich verstche nicht deutsch) "I don't understand German." It was their saying when they didn't want to answer. I heard them and told them it was a couple of miles over. I told them to get in that I would take them there. They got in the car and I ask them, what are you fellas doing? They didn't have any insignia on their uniforms like officers. They said, "We are from the United Nations, that they were there to check on the displaced Polish people, that they were going to send employees to care for them." I said, "That is what I am doing." They said, "That can't be, we don't have anyone here!" They were unaware the Polish people had been gathered up. I took them for a tour of the camp. After their tour they took out a sheet of jobs from their brief case and said, "You can pick any job you want from that job list." So instead of coming home I stayed and worked two years for the United Nations.

Not long after I had started my work I got Diphtheria. Good thing there was penicillin to arrests the disease along with lots of bed rest. I spent 6 weeks the first time in the hospital and then I went to the hotel and stayed. I check daily in at the hospital for EKGs until the end of two weeks when they said, "You've had a heart attack and have to return to the hospital." I was there another 6 weeks.

When I finally got back to work they had replaced me with an English Colonel and he didn't want me around and told me to go to the personal office. Upon my arrival, I looked around and saw all English employees. I was told to just go on and they would find something for me. I said, "I need transportation, you took my vehicle and chauffeur while I was in the hospital." There was a fella from Holland standing there and said, "We just had a Ford Station Wagon to come in that is sitting right out there." They said, "Get the keys and go on."

I just pretty much ran around for I had not received a special assignment. I had one girl to fix me up some papers so I could go to Czechoslovakia for a couple of weeks and then I went back to Salzburg. Later I went to Bolzano, Italy and stayed a couple of weeks. When I got back I took the old station wagon to have it washed, clean and the oil changed. When the charge order reach the old Colonel's desk he said, "We don't have *such* a car!" Heck, I could have sold that old wagon and got some money, for the paper work had never been done, leaving no record of it. He said, "I want to know where Lindel is?" There was a fella that spoke up and said, "I know who he is." He was sent looking for me and told me, the Colonel is looking for you! When I got to the old Colonel's office he said, "Where have you been?" I said, "You told me to go on and you'd find a job for me."

My next assignment was as Assistant Welfare Officer working with an older lady. We neither one did much. I didn't know anything about welfare. The lady in charge would check kitchens and etc. I worked for her until a fella from Washington, DC, came looking for me at the Transportation Office. He asks, "Do you like your job?" I responded that I didn't. He said, "I have a job you might like!" Cars in crates are being brought over to be assembled together. That it was about 50 miles up in the mountains at (Scutzing) Clear Lake, where there is an airplane garage where the cars can be assembled.

When I got to Clear Lake, I went to the hotel and ask for some food. The girl there said it was too late to get something to eat. I said, "I am hungry and would like to have something to eat." The boss came out and said they had a new boss coming in and that he was late. He was supposed to have been there at 1:00 p.m. and was late; that they had to keep the place clean for him. I ask them who the boss was and they said, "A man name McCullough." I said, "That is me and that I was hungry and wanted something to eat." They got me something.

I finished the car assignment up there on that cold mountain. Then, they sent me back to Salzburg to what had been a German Warehouse where medicine and different supplies were being kept. I traveled, driving into different countries; local drivers weren't allowed visas to go out of their country. They had a lot of different trucks; they had some old English trucks that the English Army had used in Africa in the earlier part of the war. They were made high up off the ground; not dual size tires, but they were the size of a Ford tractor tire. The snow was real deep on the mountain; looking down off the ledge you couldn't see daylight. I would get out using a stick to probe around for rocks. I drove two days and two nights to get to the boat docks in Trieste, Italy. They had an epidemic; no trains or airplanes could come in. I telegraphed back and found everyone at the hotel was wondering about me. I had taken a month's supply of food, two boxes matches and had filled the back of the truck with the flat 5 gallons cans full of gas to help me move around. To haul the supplies back I had to sell the gas.

In Salzburg you were unable to buy nice clothing, so while I was in Italy I went to clothing shop and picked out a nice grey, pinstriped suit. When I went to pay for the suit the fella saw I had some of those five dollar bills (scrip paper) that were no good. We were not always paid with money, sometimes they paid us with script (paper currency or a token issued) to use at PX and different places. That was what the fella wanted, I told him that they were no good, but he wouldn't take the Italy money. He thought he was going to make some money on the black market where bills were exchanged 17 bills for 1 bill. I tried to tell him the paper currency was no good, but he insisted; he handed my suit already packaged to me and as I went out the door he kept saying Goodbye-Goodbye!

I went to a ladies clothing shop and purchased some hosiery and garters that had not been available due to the war. I purchased them for the ladies at the hotel that had been so good to me while I was ill. All hosiery and garments had been banned in order to make parachutes. The soldiers would send parachutes home whenever they could to their wife, for they were made with silk.

I had a sixty day furlough to come home on leave. The sixty days didn't start until I got to DC. I went through Paris and waited around and missed the ship going over the channel. I stayed there for two weeks before going to London, England. When I got to London the girl ask if I was in a hurry to go to the United States. I said, "No!" She said to go to the office. I went to the American Embassy; I knew some marines there and stayed around the office. When I came back the ship had gone so I stayed in London for a month. I went to dog races and different things. The English people called me "Mac" for McCullough.

By that time my furlough was over. They said they were no longer sending anyone to Europe and wanted me to go to China. I went home and was told to report to Little Rock for my China Assignment. I decided not to go. The UN continued to pay me until September.

There is a young fella, Gabe Gentry that interviewed 40 veterans, including Wilbur Johnson and myself from the 250th Battalion "C" Battery. He made 10 DVDs of interviews in a project called "World War II Remembered". It is history of Arkansas veterans. One thousand copies of the documentary are to be donated to libraries and schools throughout Arkansas.

After the war I was the second person to be discharged. I had a Tec/5 rank. Fredrick from Huston, Texas and me spent two years overseas working for the United Nations. I returned to the states in 1947.

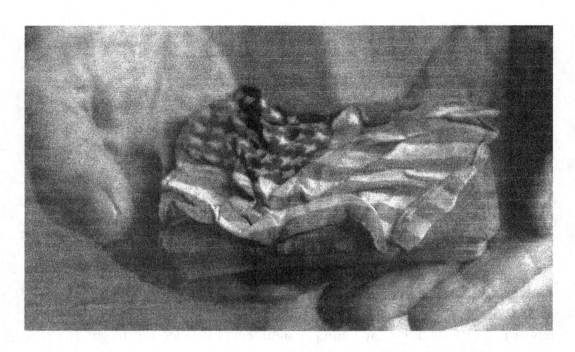

Top is the small Bible and American flag John carried in his chest pocket throughout the war in Europe. It was issued on Sept. 23, 1941, the day he reported to Ft. Sill, Oklahoma for Army duty

John J. Wann (bottom)

JOHN J. WANN

ARTILLERY B-BATTERY—LIAISON AGENT

*J*ohn was enrolled at Oklahoma State when he drafted September 23, 1941 and was sent to Ft. Sill, Oklahoma for basic training with a Horse Drawn Artillery.

From Ft. Sill, Oklahoma, John was sent to Camp Maxey, Paris, Texas for more training and assigned to the 250th Battalion.

John reflecting back over 60 years ago recollection of a long–suppressed memory from a bitterly cold Christmas eve he spent as a young Army corporal huddled in a shallow bunker in Germany. We were far from home, so young, so alone and we knew we were going to die that night on foreign soil. For John he will never forget the anguish of his best buddy pelted by shrapnel when an enemy mortar shell landed at his feet. Nine times out of ten John was right there beside Wallace. But that particular morning he wasn't.

Wallace Reid and John had promised—whoever got home first they'd go visit with the others parent. Reid having been injured got home first, but never forgot his promise he and his buddy had made. He went to see John's parents—something they never forgot.

John to this day shudders to describe the gut-wrenching drama of how his unit had to wait in formation while government-issued bulldozers pushed aside the crumpled, dead bodies of German soldiers so the U.S. jeeps could continue on their way. It was bad; it was so, so sad. Nobody should have to see anything like that. John doesn't like to go back to that time—it is just too painful. He says, "I don't talk about it much, and I don't remember it all."

It took 12½ days to cross the Atlantic in a convoy of 127 ships taking the Northern route because of *enemy* submarines. They arrived in Liverpool, England on February 23, 1944. It was cold and windy.

John remembers the invasion of Normandy, the weather, the cramped quarters while the battalion waited. It was so crowed. It was like "51 Highway" out there. He recalls the sound of enemy aircraft overhead and the sight of balloons tied to cables that U.S. troops lofted overhead to shield them from enemy attacks. It was 5-6 days, before the unit could move onto dry ground.

John remembers, to the day, how long he and fellow artillery soldiers were in battle. They took part of the destruction of the German 7th Army in the Argentan-Falaise Gap, crossed the Vosges one inch at a time for 24 hours. The mountain side was very narrow and steep. The battalion barreled into Strasbourg on Thanksgiving Day. The 250th were southeast of the "Battle of The Bugle" with General Patch's Army.

John respected General Patton and French General LeClerc (Philippe, vicomte de Hauteclocque), who commanded the 2nd French Armored Div. that fought alongside of Wann's 250th Field Artillery Battalion. He put them on the same level, the most important leaders at the time. They were something else!

General Patton liked to advance like a spearhead, moving on real fast. Sometimes we would move on so fast that the enemy had time to regroup behind us and before we knew it they'd be firing at us from the rear and we'd have to turn around and shoot—sometimes firing different directions.

Once when John, his driver and an officer were out in the jeep a buddy had gotten hurt and the medic took the jeep leaving John out there by himself. As liaison agent, John would be sent with messages to the battery commanders, for the radios weren't used behind enemy lines. John would get behind the battalion lost and then would have to find his battery. It could be pretty scary at times.

General LeClerc was an amazing strategist and motivator. He would put a group together one man at a time. At that time it was dangerous to approach anybody because you didn't know who you were talking to—it was crazy!

Thoughout the war John thoughts were of home and family. When the fighting would let up, he would relax a little. When it resumed, He said, "I prayed. When it got real bad—I prayed really hard. There was times where you did some hard thinking and praying; one thing I had to hang onto."

When I enlisted I was given a small government issued Bible and a pocket-sized silk American flag. They are the two things he really treasures and are now safely tucked in a plastic box. John traveled across France, Germany and into Austria with them in his chest pocket throughout his tour of duty in the European Theater.

For the 250th Battalion it would be 297 days, straight through, without relief. There were casualties but not like the infantry that was in front of us. I lost some good friends though. We were scared to death because we knew it could be any-one at any given time.

Sometimes, though, the pilgrimage back to 1940 when John enlisted in the army, he had joined the last remaining unit of the horse-drawn mounted cavalry before everything became motorized. Once while riding a horse pulling a cart reel with communication wire, John got a whip lash and was in the hospital a week. The ground was rough and the fast speed all compound the problem.

One day John strapped on a German pistol, holster and other seized trappings for a photograph to send home when his commanding officer walk past and with a firm order, "get that stuff off you right now!" The picture is John clad in army brown breeches, knee-high leather boots and a smile of a young man having some fun.

John recalls, "I rolled my pant legs past the knees and waded into a German river to scavenge fish killed upstream where other soldiers had tossed grenades into the river for a sport. They would kill the fish, but we would be down stream to get them. My buddies and I cleaned a pile of sandfish on the creek bank with a bottle of wine."

The 250th fired their last round near Munich. The battalion was in bivouac on the northern edge of the German Alps in Austria when word came May 8, 1945, that victory had been declared.

While in Austria there were two little boys that John and other soldiers befriended that played in the area they were assigned. Their names were Hans and Walter. As they grew, perhaps, it was through these children's eye that the past could best be told how the "American soldiers" befriended them.

John came home on a boat called "Vulcania". He returned home—mustered out of Camp Chaffee near Ft. Smith, AR, November 6, 1945. John had promised his parents he would be home in time for Thanksgiving. He had been given a physical and the doctors wanted to put him in the hospital. John said he would go home and come back later. They told John it was either go to the hospital or sign out—John signed out. Leaving behind were the strains, the stresses of time spent in France and Germany.

John's story was revised from a Veteran's Day article from the Madison County Journal, a local newspaper with some addition from my talking to John. It was a touching story to write.

*Hdq. Battery Men: Milton Broussard is in the **center of second row** (wearing two helmets);
Jeff Hackler is on the **lower right corner** holding his helmet; Arthur Goe is **standing directly back of Jeff***
PICTURE: COURTESY OF JORAYNE HACKLER

ARTHUR GOE

HEADQUARTERS: WIREMAN

After my inducting at Little Rock Arkansas in 1943, I was sent to Camp Maxey, Paris, Texas. Our training consisted of preparing us to be good soldiers. From Camp Maxey we were sent for maneuvers in Louisiana and then back to Camp Maxey for more training—soon to be shipped out for overseas duty.

We departed Camp Maxey by train for New York, and then we were sent to Camp Shanks, New Jersey. The battalion left from New York on February 11, 1944 on a British ship, Dominion Monarch crossing the Atlantic in the dark, rainy mixed with sleet night. We were on the Dominion Monarch for 12 and 1/2 days.

On the ship for breakfast they fed us boiled sausage, bread and butter and something we thought was coffee. We learned later it was tea with cream.

A fella from Headquarters, Leroy Kunshick, from Austin, Texas got sick and we had shang haied him to a hospital back in Paris, Texas. Some of us fellas went to visit him at the hospital before we left. They were getting the battalion ready to ship us overseas. Meanwhile, before our embarkation somebody had gotten Leroy out of the hospital; he didn't want us going overseas without him. The Atlantic was rough and Leroy was seasick all the way overseas—just one of many men! Leroy was known for his eating, but never ate anything while on ship and layover in a corner. He lost weight, but once we got on land he was ok. They never knew what was wrong with him in the hospital in Paris, Texas. Big (Tarzan) Leroy was a good friend of Charles Wade.

On February 23rd we arrived in Liverpool, England and then by train we were taken to Atherstone, England. The darnedest thing, though, before they would unload us at Liverpool, the English had to have their tea.

While we were at Atherstone the cooks were working out of a 25ft. across and 12-14 deep place feeding 500 men out of the whole kitchen. On Saturday the cooks prepared chicken and gravy and then warmed it up the next morning. It was served with fruit cocktail. When they open up a new pot of the chicken and gravy you could smell it. All over there was a bunch of men sick. Everyone had shovels digging a trench toilet and then, they covered up any human feces. I washed my pan *real* good!

From Southampton, England the 250th Battalion boarded the U.S.S. Herkimer for Normandy, France—soon to be amidst the war.

In one area our wire section bivouacs near a creek. We put our tents down in a swale. It rained making the creek rise and it got our entire bedroll wet. It got wet from the creek rising, not from the rain.

Once, two of our men, James Cox and Sergeant Elwyn Allen, had disappeared. When they came back they had 30-40 Germans in a German truck—that was what saved them from a possible court-martial!

After the war Headquarters were billeted to a castle in Glanegg, Austria. I came home early for a 30 day leave; the plans were to go on to Japan. There were six of us that left Salzburg: Clifford Britt, James Cox, Joe Bradshaw and myself plus two other men. We were sent to Oberammegau, Germany where we went into replacement camp for 4-5 days. At Oberammegau every 10 years Germany has a "Passion Play" for the whole town up in the mountains. Once every ten years, at the start if a new decade, local residents of Oberammergau's small town of Germany perform the Passionsspiele (Passion play), a dramatic recreation of the last days of Christ. It is one of Germany's oldest festivals.

Then we got on a 40-8; a boxcar—meaning 40 men or 8 horses. From Oberammegau we were sent to Lucky Strike Camp and from there we went to

New York and to Camp Shanks for one night. We were out on the train dock at Utica, New York when we heard a conductor say the war was over. We had dropped the two bombs on Japan bringing the war to an end.

The American Legion has an organization called 40-8. It is an inverted diamond with a horizontal line under the 40 with an 8 beneath. We men did have fun!

Ralph Phillips
Ralph fixing himself some coffee....It was close to end of the war and everyone was afraid.

Ralph Phillips

HEADQUARTERS' BATTERY: LT. TOOLEN'S ASSISTANT

I arrived at Camp Maxey, Paris, Texas in January 30, 1944 for basic training. Then it was on for maneuvers in Louisiana and back to Camp Maxey for more training; they were getting ready to ship the battalion overseas. January 30, 1944 by train we were sent to New York and arrived at Camp Shanks, New Jersey on February 2nd. On February 9th we left the New York Harbor on the Dominion Monarch for a 12 and 1/2 day trip crossing the Atlantic Ocean. It was the largest troop movement out of New York for overseas duty. We arrived in Liverpool, England February 23rd, and from there we were sent to Atherstone. It was from Atherstone to Shelfield and back to Atherstone. Then we next were sent to Somybridge, Wales on May 8th back to Atherstone on June 6th. It was just from one place to another. On June the 9th the battalion was sent to Swanwick, England and on to Lobscombe on July 18th; the same day we arrived in Southampton, England. The battalion embarked from Old Docks, Southampton where we boarded the U.S.S. Herkimer on the 19th and arrived on the Utah Beach on the 23rd of July.

We fought from the pubs in England to Austria where it would all end with the battalion setting records. We went through 27 cities crossing France and 24 cities in Germany.

The first airfield we captured in France in July 1944 there was the Fw190 (Jerry) airplane in the hanger. I tried to start it or pull in out of the hanger without any success.

The Fw190 first met in action with the British "RAF" in the spring of 1941. It was superior to the RAFs latest "Spitfire". The Fw190 was powered by a BMW 801Dg two-row radial, rated at 1600hp or 1700hp, it was smaller than any British fighter, yet carried more armament, four 20mm cannon and two machine guns. It was unsurpassed maneuverability, well-protected, and had a wide track landing gear. New versions appeared types with heavier armament torpedo bombers, dual-control trains, and night fighters. The Fw190G had fewer guns and carried a fantastic bomb, rocket, or torpedo load up to a few thousand pounds. The landing gear had been strengthened and it carried rockets to use against Allied ground forces or bombers. Fw190D, or long nosed 190, was the fastest of all versions. It had a Jumo 213A liquid-cooled engine. Designer Kurt Tank use his own name and had it applied to the final development, the Ta152 with even a higher performance. Total Fw190s produced was 20,051 aircraft. Fortunately, for the Allied that there were only a handful of the Ta152 that Tank was testing when our P-51 Mustang started to dominate the skies. The Mustangs with Packard-Merlin engine made it the most efficient, fastest Allied fighter in World War II. The Ta152, when the throttle was opened our Allied fighters were unable to get near it. With both the lack of fuel capacity and untrained pilots the Ta152 were often unable to fly—a design change that benefited the United States.

We were men all in the same boat. We took care of each other. There was a boy named Moberly from Florida who was only fifteen years old. We were firing across the Danube River when his mother finally had tracked him down. The night before he was to leave for home, Moberly took every man's turn on the guns. That's the way we were—helping one another.

Once when we were having a counter-battery I went diving beneath a truck—of all places to go! I broke two fingers when they went into the ground as I was trying to get beneath the truck. I had to wear braces on the two fingers for awhile.

While in around the Blue Danube there were Germans all over—I said,

"Hell with the war!" I went fishing and deer hunting. I got both, some fish and a deer. I shot the deer, but I used a German grenade "potato masher" to catch the fish. The German grenade looked like a tin can with a handle resembling a potato masher.

My duties called for my working close to Lt. Toolen; what was called his (Dog Robber). I took care of and watched out for Toolen and the other observers when they were around. I also would go out on liaison observation post assignments. Lt. Toolen flew an L-4 Piper Club 1,500ft. dodging bullets… dangerous missions! Lts.' Cozort and Toolen were liaison pilots; Frazer and Jarabowski were observers. There were 68,560 rounds of ammunition fired by the Battalion during the war.

Toolen, an Irishman, liked his liquor. On November 20th, Lt. Toolen's airplane was turned over from high windstorm near the Vosges Mountains. While grounded, Toolen and a member of the French Air Segment made a trip to a nearby village to get some cognac. While there, they were told about there being some German soldiers up in the hills that wanted to surrender, but not to the French. Service Battery had stayed behind to coordinate the supplies. Captain High of Service Battery was contacted and asked to receive and take care of them. Captain High disarmed them and then called for MP's to get and move them to a POW stockade.

It was around Baccarat—Luneville area that it rained for 26 days. What a mess! Baccarat, France is where they made beautiful crystal. There had been a large German garrison in the area before it was liberated.

Toolen was in 176 combat missions as a Liaison Pilot and received 25 decorations. Toolen had no living relatives, not even a cousin. He willed a goodly sum of money to his Alma Mater, Michigan State University. His name is displayed in raised letters in the Kellogg Building.

After the war was over and time to come home, I was sent to Camp Phillip Morris, France. From Camp Phillip Morris I boarded the Le Cross Victory ship sail bound for home. I arrived in Kilmer, New Jersey and discharged from the Jefferson Barracks in Missouri.

Ralph Phillips was the one responsible with getting the whole 250th Battalion together. The first reunion was formed in 1964. A Mrs. Deckard was a telephone operator at the time, and at night she made it a duty to locate those of B-Battery, which helped Ralph upfront in forming the reunion. The 250th is grateful for *all* that Ralph has done.

Russell W. Milliken presented Ralph with a 250th plaque for his dedicated work organizing the 250th FABn Reunion. The first reunion was held in 1964.

Copy of a charcoal done in Paris, France of Thomas (T.O.) Johnson—1945

Thomas Oscar (T.O.) Johnson

ARTILLERY B-BATTERY: CHIEF OF GUN SECTION

T.O. served with the 250th Battalion as Chief of Section, which served in the European Theater during World War II. The battalion earned 5 battle stars, one each for each campaign: Normandy; Northern France; Rhineland; Central European; Ardennes-Alsace, plus, arrowhead for amphibious landing.

The 250th received the U. S. Government for Meritorious Achievement. The 250th Field Artillery Battalion was recognized for being the first artillery battalion to fire around of ammunition across the Rhine River into Germany; honor given by firing the one-millionth round of ammunition across the Rhine in the XV Corps. On January 29th, 1945 at 1430 a brief ceremony was held with generals and colonels present: Brigadier General John B. Murphy, Gunner—100th Division Artillery; Brigadier General Edward S. Ott, XV Corps Artillery #1; Colonel Eric A. Erickson, 200th Field Artillery group #2: Lt. Colonel W. K. Jealous, 250th Field Artillery Battalion #3.

General Ott sent the shell hurdling into Bitche with T. O. Johnson's gun of B-Battery firing the millionth round at Citadel Bitche, France. Each round of artillery was recorded.

T. O. was one of several from the 250th Battalion to return in 1979 to Europe to retrace the path that was taken with both the 3rd and the 7th Armies during

World War II across France, Germany and then on into Austria.

T.O. Johnson was a soldier in every way. He was quite a gentleman who is truly missed.

T.O. Johnson & Brigadier General Edward Ott

Site of one-millionth round of ammunition fired across the Rhine River. Brigadier General S. Edward Ott sent the shell hurling into Bitche with T.O. Johnson's gun of B-Battery at Citadel Bitche, France.

WWII/KOREA/VIETNAM

LECILE WIX

Lecile Wix served proudly with the 250th FABn during World War II.
PICTURE: COURTESY OF LECILE'S SONS: TOM, TED AND MIKE

LECILE WIX

*L*ecile was just shy of eighteen when he visited his Aunt and Uncle at Fort Benning, Georgia. Lecile's Aunt was married to a fellow that was a Master Sergeant in the Army. Lecile decided he wanted to join the army. Uncle Oliver Tubbs tried to talk him out of it and said, "If you get in my platoon you will be sorry—I will be harder on you than the rest because of our relationship." Sure enough, Lecile was assigned to "tough" Uncle Tubbs! Lecile said, "It was hard—no partiality was shown."

Lecile was one of the cadre members sent to Camp Maxey, Paris, Texas for the activation and formation of the 250th Field Artillery Battalion.

After much training, the battalion was being prepared for overseas duty. Lecile suggested to Dottie to go home for she was expecting their first baby in five months.

Dottie and Evelyn Cagle left Paris, Texas traveling by train. There were two soldiers setting right behind them that had seen Lecile and Peter Cagle. To Evelyn and Dottie they said, "Well, you two going home before you become widows?" The GIs said the battalion was to ship out in two or three days; that they were already packed to go.

In Texarkana Dottie took a bus to Birmingham and Evelyn went to Georgia.

At Birmingham Dottie's family picked her up and took her home to Cullman. As soon as they got home, Dottie called Lecile saying, "I am going to get a flight back." Lecile said, "Don't come, for I may not even be here!" Lecile never told Dottie ahead of time, but Dottie thought Evelyn knew.

Dottie never heard from Lecile for 2-3 weeks. He had left Camp Maxey to Camp Shanks, New York bound for Europe. Lecile was the 250th Battalion Supply Sergeant and was part of the advance detail group that was sent ahead to Europe. He went overseas on the Queen Elizabeth, no escort and was in Liverpool, England, in five days.

Lecile never spoke much about the war years—just little bits here and there. He did mention about he was traveling with his supply men and came upon an American road block and Lecile wanted to get through to get to the unit ahead. The Lieutenant said, "You don't want to go around that curve because there is a German road block." The lieutenant was what saved them.

Another time, he recalled, one night while the 250th Battalion was moving, they noticed some stuff along the road side. At daybreak, they saw there were a bunch of German bodies. They had traveled through a battle area without any knowledge.

Lecile reenlisted in June 1950, at the time of the Korean War. He went in as a reservist (member of the Military Reserve) in September 1950, in October was sent for active military duty. He served in Vietnam, was stationed in Japan, South France and twice in Alaska. CWO/4 Wix retired January 1, 1971.

Thanks to Dottie Wix for her help to write Lecile's story. Lecile and Dottie both have passed away. Lecile having spent 10 years in a veteran's facility in Alabama died on August 9, 2006. Dottie died in 2007. It was not expected.

A verse spoken by daughter, Diane, and son, Tom, at Lecile's memorial:

Do not stand at my grave and weep;
I am not there, I do not sleep.
I am a thousand winds that blow.
I am the diamond's gilt on snow.

I am the sunlight on ripened grain.
I am the gentle autumn's rain.
When you awake in the morning's hush,
I am the sweet uplifting rush,
Of quite birds in circle flight—
I am the soft stars that shine at night.
Do not stand at my grave and cry,
I am not here, I did not die.

The funeral was lovely, which included children, Tom, Ted, Mike, Diane and [Diane's husband] Ronald Finch words of tribute to their *beloved* father and father–in law. Ted after he spoke turned and saluted his father [Ted served with his father in Vietnam], leaving a breathtaking moment.

Before the funeral service a down pour came. Luckily, the rain stopped, the skies cleared for a helicopter to fly over coming in from the southeast and returned coming from the south to making a V [>]—what a moving few minutes! It was as if the Lord withheld the rain for the delivery of that joyful moment of Lucile's departure. It was so inspiring.

Ted still flies a helicopter as a lifeline pilot. Mike, also, served his country as Ted and his father. Tom having lost an eye as a small child prevented him from serving. Daughter, Diane, served in a capacity where she had to use a secret clearance pass.

Charles F. Dalferes (top)

Charles Dalferes's gun crew in training at Camp Maxey (bottom)

Charles F. Dalferes

Artillery A-Battery: 105 mm Howitzer Gunner

Along with the greeting from Uncle Sam, I went in at Christmas as all the rest did. I remained an A-Battery gunner throughout the war regardless of never being able to keep my "Corporal" stripes! I was Captain Howard Leslie's problem child. I loved to party and go places and still to this day I'm the same except that now I'm my wife's problem child. We all went through the same battles, fears, prayers and miseries. I wish I had never seen the concentration camp (Dachau), for it left an indelible horror in my mind that haunts my dreams still to this day. The funny incidents kept us going and sane. At one of our dinners in the edge of a forest, Colonel Jealous found out we were the only Battery with coffee. He was having coffee with Captain Leslie when a German 88 shell came squealing over and land close to the front wheel of our mess truck where they were talking. Everyone froze! It was a "DUD" and a voice said, "Well, Leslie, if that is all you wanted to see me about, come on driver lets go." After the tension subsided, we all enjoyed the episode.

Charles corresponded to his Mother and wife, Amelia, through poems pretty much of the time. Regretfully, Amelia lost most of the poems sent to her through storage.

This poem was written to his mother in November 22, 1944.

    Somewhere
It's getting late,
    And everything is still.
For this I wait,
    To dream of you—I will.

In shivering cold
    I hear you say,
Son, behold,
    In your heart I'll stay.
In smothering heat
    I hear you say,
Take pride, my son,
    We can't be beat!

In my loneliness I have consolation,
    It's not for me, but for our nation.
Away from you I was carried off,
    But you will agree that God is our boss.

Only last night
    I silently prayed,
For you and my loved ones'
    Memories never fade.

The noise of battle is far away
    Where I wish truly it would stay.
But after this brief period of rest,
    Again, we'll go do our best.

For your sincere prayers
    Is all I ask?
Wait! For the end of this poem
    'Til we end our task.

On October 4, 1945 while in Belgium Charles wrote this poem for his beloved Amelia. P.O.E.: Port of Embarkation.

Two days from hence,
    I'll be beyond this "Ripple Dapple" fence.
To a P.O.E. unknown,
    From where to you…
I'll always be flown.
    To you, I say—for—"you"
To me, is Home!

Celebrating their anniversary—2001

I, personally, took this picture for I have *never* seen a bubblier couple. They are always like this. Their love for one another just shines through. Charles is a very good pianist and vocalist, but with having throat cancer he no longer can sing. Charles is fighting a battle with cancer just as he did during the war—with laughter and enjoying himself to the fullest. He is a winner!

Charles and Amelia were hit hard with Katrina, but with a strong determination and with daughter, Diane's love, care and help, they are back into their home. It isn't like it once was, but it is home. Just as Vincent and Dora Colombo, they never gave up and kept on smiling even though Charles has had some hospital stays—may God bless them!

Jeff D. Hackler and Gene Baker at Camp Lucky Strike, France, where the saga ends

JEFF D. HACKLER

HEADQUARTERS' BATTERY: SWITCHBOARD OPERATOR

*T*here were two brothers from Mountain Home that served during World War II in different parts of Europe. Jeff served with the 250th Field Artillery Battalion Headquarters, and Joe Bill was in the Air Corps, as bombardier and navigator. Joe did not serve with the 250th Battalion. The Air Corps is now the U.S. Air Force.

Jeff is deceased and his wife, Jorayne, wrote some things down about Jeff and sent articles about Jeff's brother Joe.

Jeff left from Little Rock, Arkansas, as many other young men, to Camp Maxey, Paris, Texas for combat training. From Camp Maxey the 250th was sent to Louisiana for Army maneuvers and then back to Camp Maxey. They were getting the battalion ready for overseas duty. From Camp Maxey the 250th Battalion left by train for New York and on to Camp Shanks.

While assigned to Camp Shanks, Jeff and C.A. Britt went to Jack Dempsey's Bar and to the Waldorf Astoria, as far as the lobby—they did enjoy the night in town.

They left the New York Harbor on a British ship that took them to Liverpool,

England. Jeff talked about the food on board the Dominion Monarch and being so seasick.

After arriving in Liverpool, England they went on to Atherstone to the Atherstone estate of Sir William Dugdale where some of the batteries were assigned. They were told to dig foxholes, and Sir William Dugdale's caretakers objected. Their Headquarters' C.O. took care of that!

Jeff was proud of the 250th Field Artillery record and had spoken with great pride of their firing the first artillery round across the Rhine River into Germany and their supporting the French 2nd Armored Division command by General LeClerc at Strasbourg.

Jeff took his R&R in Nancy, France and went on into Paris. Jorayne recalls, "Jeff, while in Paris bought me a beautiful bracelet, but found that he bought a piece of junk! The bracelet would turn when worn. We took it to a jeweler and was told it wasn't worth having it gold plated."

After VE-Day Jeff ended up at Camp Lucky Strike, France where it would be his departure for home.

Jeff's brother, Joe, was a 26 year old officer. On his last mission, his plane had just moved into lead position and was hit immediately by German antiaircraft guns. It exploded in a violent blast that blew the nose of the plane (where Joe sat) and the tail of the plane (where the tail gunner sat) into hostile skies. He can't recall exactly how he managed to get out of the wreckage to pull his parachute ripcord. Only 1,000 feet from the ground, his chute opened, and he hit the ground hard, injuring his knees and legs. Joe was captured and listed as missing-in-action, but later escaped. For three months he walked more than 250 miles on injured legs. Joe and another crew member, Dale Morrison, were the only survivors of the 10-man crew. On an earlier mission when his plane went down, he was able to save his crew, but he was badly burned.

Jeff had been getting letters from Joe, then no letters at all. Jeff knew before Jorayne wrote him that Joe's plane had been hit. During this time, Lt. Richard Bump was supportive and kind to Jeff. A lasting friendship would grow between the two out of Jeff's grief for his brother. Luckily, the two brothers both would make it home.

After 58 years Joe Bill received the "Distinguished Flying Cross" medal award. Joe doesn't want to be called a hero, but that's what he has become to his hometown people. "It was nothing, just standard," Joe says about the Purple Heart. He earned three Oak Leaf Clusters on the Purple Heart. He also won an award for a parachute jump over enemy territory. Upon receiving his "Distinguished Flying Cross" specifically for his actions on his 39th mission, Joe was given three standing ovations. It overwhelmed him. When he accepted the award, Joe said. "But when I think about those eight boys who perished, 10 missions later, it humbles me. I got to go home. They (his very tight knit crew) paid the supreme price of war." Speaking of those that didn't make it. Joe served 49 dangerous missions during World War II. A story that went untold for 58 years ... long time for *such* bravery! Joe was elected for two terms to the Arkansas House of Representatives from Baxter County. In 1980, he was elected as a delegate to the Arkansas Constitutional Convention.

The 250th men had a special affection for Colonel Jealous and Mrs. Jealous. It is a great tribute to a man that stands right up there with the best! Lt. and Mrs. Dorothea Bump visited Jeff and Jorayne in Arkansas many times. Mr. and Mrs. Bump were from Muncie, Indiana.

Louis J. Cunningham

LOUIS J. CUNNINGHAM

A-BATTERY: ARTILLERY 1ST GUNNER CREW

When Louis came back to the United States to civilian life, he set off to continue his life as a young southern Louisiana man. He was always proud of his time served in the Army during World War II. He held his chin out when he would speak of his army buddies from the 250th FABn. He did not make it a common practice to tell stories of his memories of the war. On rare occasions, he would offer stories about the more lighthearted events and times during his tour of duty in Europe. As far as the truly heroic efforts displayed by Louis and his brothers in the 250th, and the sights and sounds that lived on in their collective memory, those memories, evidently were just too hard to speak of the many taunting moments.

In summary of his service with the 250th Field Artillery Battalion, Louis J. Cunningham was a member of "A" Battery: Artillery 1st Gunner. The 250th was a light artillery battalion assigned to augment the divisional artillery as support and /or direct fire. The 250th and others like it that were often attached to different "Parent" groups as the need for more artillery was required in certain battleground conditions. It has been said that the record of the 250th Field Artillery Battalion is so amazing and colorful that probably no other artillery has been before or since close to it.

The battalion served under some very distinguished leaders. French General LeClerc referred to the 250th as his "Automatic Artillery". So proficient were their firing skills (jacket training record) of the 250th Battalion, George Patton chose it to be a charter member of his newly formed 3rd Army. The 250th served under General Patch who commanded 7th Army, as well as General Haislip's XV Corps. The 250th would serve 297 consecutive days in combat without relief, fighting across France, Germany and into Austria until the end of the war in Europe. The Battalion was awarded many commendations and citations from divisions they supported. "Of these citations," daughter Gena says, "the one Daddy treasured the most was the "Lorraine Cross" awarded to them by the French Army."

Brigadier General Edwards S. Scott was quoted while praising the 250th Battalion, "Not once did you request or complain of your assignment." As a separate light field artillery battalion, assigned to the XV Corps, they were constantly being attached to one unit or another, but always where the fire power was needed the most, and where the fighting was the hottest.

Charles Dalferes was a howitzer gunner with "A" Battery. Louis served as a cannoneer for Charles.

Louis returned from the war at Christmas time. He met his future wife Della Theriot shortly after and they married on March 10, 1946. Louis Cunningham lived a long happy life with Della their three daughters, one son and grandchildren. But he still had another battle to fight; this time it was cancer. After a hard fight, Louis passed away on April 14, 2004 at the age of 82. He was raised a country boy, and learned to work hard to make a life for his family by doing what was required of him. Louis was employed by Texaco for 30 years where he worked as 1st mate on a tugboat; he also was a crane operator during his years of Texaco employment.

Louis Cunningham would not be forgotten by his beloved daughter, Gena, who has compiled a 32 page booklet in honor of her father's service with the 250th Field Artillery Battalion in World War II. Louis would be *most proud* of her endeavor. This article has Gena's own thoughts of her father's loyalty to his country and family.

Chester Blaylock standing by the machine gun. The "Heavy Machine" Battery orders were for the gunner's to stand at their gun at Dachau, for it was thought there may be a possible air bombing. This interesting picture was provided by Chester Blaylock.

CHESTER BLAYLOCK

HEADQUARTERS: HEAVY MACHINE GUNNER

I was drafted and entered the army in 1941 and assigned with the 250th Headquarters' Operations and Maintenance as a 50 caliber heavy machine gunner, the 50 caliber was used mainly for firing at aircraft. I remember our going through the Falaise Gap and the Vosges Mountains and mentioned that no artillery before them had ever attempted crossing the Vosges. They were known to be very dangerous mountains. About half way through the Vosges we were surprised to see a German soldier on the roadside. Captain Milligan got out to check and found it was just a young boy about 15 years old dressed in a large German uniform. He had been injured and Captain Milligan called back for a medic up front. They got a stretcher and put the boy on it and immediately started ripping off the German uniform from the boy's leg. When they lanced the wound a piece of metal artillery shell popped out and I picked it up and looked at it. The boy was cleaned up and clean clothes put on him. Captain Milligan (the great person he was) said, "Sonny Boy! You may lose your leg, but I think we saved your life."

There were some boys sent from New York that trained our squad. They did all the figuring out for us (they were like our computers we use today) and knew what they were doing.

Captain Milligan was a grand person. He told us, "I want you to know—we have young men here, many don't have an education. I am going to need your full attention, for when we leave here be real careful what you say or do for any of us can go out there and lose a ship or battle right to the higher up." If we had been told to jump off the wall we would have.

At Dachau I was told where to stand with my machine gun (picture), for there was some concern of a possible air bombing. The smoke stack was still smoking. The last person sent into the crematorium was a mother and little child—a terrible thing for everyone to see! The SS troops had walked those poor people around till they were worn out and then they were loaded onto a train and brought to Dachau. There was a railroad track that went right into the crematorium. They would send the poor souls in for a bath, but instead to a gas chamber.

After VE-Day everyone was split into two groups. I was reassigned to the 208th Field Artillery Battalion. Long toms had been loaded on ships bound for the Pacific when President Truman had the two bombs dropped ending the war in the Pacific. I wouldn't have to go to the Pacific, but would return home with a Corporal rank.

Chester is standing next to the howitzer shells lying on the ground to his right.

Little Vincent Colombo, Jr., (photo right)
PICTURE: COURTESY OF JOHN AND DOT WANN

Vincent Colombo, Jr.

I was drafted at age 20 and inducted into the Army on December 19, 1942, and was sent on by train to Camp Beauregard, LA and arrived there that night. Upon reporting to Camp Beauregard, first thing was roll call and then we were issued our clothing and assigned to KP duty. Those that were in charge at Camp Beauregard ask for six volunteers to go to Alexandria in an army truck. Of course, I volunteered thinking it was a good deal at the time. We marched about a half mile to the motor pool. Upon our arrival there we quickly learned we had been tricked. The motor pool had wheelbarrows, and we were instructed to move coal to each storage hut outside of each barracks until they were filled. It was very cold. Boy! That was the last I ever volunteered for anything.

We stayed at Camp Beauregard for two days until we were transferred to Camp Maxey, Paris, Texas where we were assigned to the 250th Field Artillery Battalion. At Camp Maxey we had 13 weeks of basic training and maneuvers in Louisiana. It was at Maxey that I was assigned Captain High's driver and would remain his driver all across France into Germany and into Salzburg, Austria. After basic training we were sent by train to Camp Shanks, New York for a few days, and then orders were issued to gather our equipment to board the Dominion Monarch ship for Liverpool, England. It would take 12½ days to cross the North Atlantic

Ocean, and all the while the giant conglomeration of ship convoys zigzagged trying to avoid the enemy submarines. We arrived in Liverpool, England and stayed overnight before moving on to Atherstone. From there we would leave for maneuvers and wouldn't return until orders were received to go to Southhampton. We stayed at Southampton for a week loading supplies on a truck and then drove it down to the ship for loading. When we got to the port they picked up the whole truck and put it onto the ship. We crossed over the English Channel to Normandy Beach and drop anchor. We arrived 44 days after D-Day at Utah Beach. The waters were too swift and we stayed on ship until the waters calmed, and then we unloaded onto trucks and went ashore. We saw a lot of devastation all along the beachhead left from earlier invasions. That night we bivouac at an apple orchard where there were several gas alarms. I didn't get any sleep. I was scared, and kept in hand my rosary and prayed.

The next day we went through St. Lô where the fighting had been heavy. It had been heavily bombed. We moved on through those awful hedgerows that one could never forget! General Patton would arrive on July 31, 1943. We had been assigned to his 3rd Army. On August 1, we started at the Avanches Gap moving on through Fougeres, Lemans onto Argentan to Falaise Gap where there was a bloody battle.

Patton kept us moving at a fast pace. We moved onto Mantes and outside of Paris where we ran out of gas and had to sit for a week. At the Dompaire and Luneville area, we were transferred to the 7th Army after 56 days with General Patton. The Seventh Army was commanded by General Patch. The 250th under the command of General Haislip's XV Corps moved through the Vosges Mountains and on into Strasbourg under the command of French General LeClerc. The Vosges Mountains were very dangerous mountains. It was thought no one could cross them, but we went through fast and was in Strasbourg on Thanksgiving Day. The 7th Army was the first to reach the Rhine River, but was sent back because the Battle of the Bulge. We wouldn't cross the Rhine until March 26th of 1945.

We left Strasbourg and moved onto the Rahling/Bitche area where we stayed for two months. We were snow bound. We would burn trees and steno and wore lots of clothing. It was cold. I would lay on the front seat of the jeep because I am so short and could fit there. After the snow melted, we would move on to assault the Siegfried line moving toward Zweibrücken. At Worms we crossed the river over into Germany on pontoon bridges. After *several* more towns we moved into Dachau's unbelievable and unforgettable sight. Upon leaving Dachau's horror, our battalion moved on to the outskirts of Munich where the fighting would all end. From Munich we drove on to the beautiful town of Salzburg, Austria by truck.

At Berchtesgaden, Hitler had built this long tunnel that took you to a large room. It looked to be a conference room where they would meet—what a sight!

Finally, on May 8, Lt. Colonel Jealous announced the war was over in Europe. To celebrate VE-Day the men drank, sing and danced with the girls. A few of the men brought the girls back home with them. I happen to get sick the night of the celebration. I went looking for the fella only to find him passed out in a flower pot. That was a funny sight to see.

We stayed at an old brewery for a month at Grodig, Austria. We mustered out according to points. You'd get different points for things you accomplished or ribbons you had received and amount of time where spent.

We drove through the Alps in the truck down to Marseilles, France. That night I went to take a shower and it was about a block from the barracks. I almost froze to death in the shower because it was so cold. I woke up the next morning with a fever. Medical personal told me I had a virus and a Frenchman made me a hot toddy (drink consisting of liquor rum, water, sugar, and spices). I felt much better the next morning—I believe that hot toddy did the trick! I received my orders I could go home. It took six days to get to Norfolk, VA. Seven days less than when we went overseas. I got back on December 19, 1945. I was gone 3 years and 3 days. When our ship docked a taxi cab was waiting by the ship, and he told us fellas he would take us to New Orleans for $50. a person. The five of us jumped at the price. In New Orleans the cab dropped me off on Franklin Ave., and then I took a cab to Arabi to my sister's house. She ran down the steps she was so excited to see me. We were hugging each other and crying.

Vincent would return home as a Tech 5. He was one of twenty to receive the French Croix de Guerre Medals and one of one hundred that received a Bronze Star Medal as well as other medals.

At Camp Maxey Vincent was first assigned as a cook. He later was reassigned to serve as driver for Captain High of Service Battery. When he was around Headquarters, Lt. Colonel Jealous would have "Little Vincent" drive him around although he had his own personal driver. Vincent is only 5 ft. tall.

Vincent was referred to as "Battery Agent" or "Runner". He carried a gun, but never used it. He had dangerous jobs at times. He spent 50% of the time driving by himself. He'd drive convoys; drive to get mail, checks or drive 50 miles to ration trucks to get supplies. He'd drive blackout at night. Drivers had to keep a watchful alert with readiness for the dangerous wire that the Germans had strung out. The wire was razor sharp, and if you drove into one, it would cut a person's head right off. The St. Lo hedgerow shielded the Germans; it was the most dangerous place to hit the strung wire. It was the breakthrough for the Normandy invasion. The fighting was ferocious.

As a side note: Vincent took his very own pillow from home with him when he went to war and would keep it in a duffle bag. He used "his home away from home keepsake" every night. It returned home with him and remained with him until Hurricane Katrina. The German Lugar, 2 swords and two daggers mementoes he got home with after the World War II he still has. His son's were able to go in and retrieve them, but his army pictures were destroyed. Hurricane's Katrina and Rita *took so much* and *left so little* for some. Vincent and Dora along with three other families of the 250th Field Artillery Battalion, Charles and Amelia Dalferes, Walter and Rosie Yuratich and Mrs. Lucreia Everhardt lives were changed forever. Vincent and Dora never got back into their home until the middle of 2007 with work to still be done. But you never hear them complain—what a gift!

The precious couple would meet after the war and marry. They were blessed with four lovely children. They shall never be forgotten for their beautiful dancing. While dancing at the 250th Reunions', couples would step off the dance floor just to watch Vincent and Dora's graceful dance floor moves....

Vincent & Dora at the 1st FABn Reunion held in 1964 (top)
PICTURE: COURTESY OF RALPH PHILLIPS

Picture Author took at the 2003 FABn Reunion (bottom)

Loran K. Rutledge at Rome, Italy on a 10-day pass—1945

Loran K. Rutledge

103rd Infantry Division: Heavy Machine Gunner

*W*hen I was in the first semester of my senior year at Crawfordsville High School, I was asked to meet with Walter Spencer, Chairman of the Selective Service Board.

Mr. Spencer told me if I signed up to go into the service at the time and had a passing grade in the first six weeks of the second semester I would receive my diploma. I check with my parents and they agreed. I left for the Army on the February 5, 1944, and received my diploma while in combat in France.

I reported for duty on the 5th of February at Fort Benjamin Harrison, and shipped to Camp Blanding, Florida for basic training. After completion of basic training my MOS was a machine gunner in a heavy weapons company.

I left Camp Blanding, Florida to report to Camp Shanks, New York. Since I was only 18 years old I was too young to go overseas. I was shipped out to Camp Claiborne, Louisiana for more training for six weeks.

In the summer of 1944 I was transferred to Camp Howze, Texas where I joined the 103rd Infantry Division. I was assigned to Company D 410 Infantry Regiment. The 103rd was ordered overseas where we went to Camp Shanks, NY for deployment. We arrived in Marseilles, France on October 15, 1944. I was only 18 years of age but turned 19, sixteen days later.

We entered combat in November of 1944 and was assigned to the 7th Army under the command of General Patch. Upon entering combat we had to cross a flooded Meurth River at St. Die, France. It took us all night to cross the pontoon bridge. After crossing the river we stayed in a barn until day light—we were officially in combat.

By being new to combat we made several mistakes. Firing at anything that moved caused us to give away our position. On the 3rd or 4th day we were moving up a hill when we became pinned down by mortar fire by a German sniper on our right and left flank. Sgt. Plummer, 1st heavy machine gunner, got hit in the foot with a round.

General Haffner, the Commanding General of the 103rd Infantry Division and CEO of RR Donnelley Co., became ill and was rotated back to the states. General McAuliffe of the 101st. Division took over his command told the Germans at Bastogne (Battle of the Bulge) they were nuts after they had asked him to surrender.

When the Battle of Bastogne took place the 103rd Division of the 7th Army was on the right flank of the 7th Army. We were then transferred to the left flank of the 7th Army or the right flank of the 3rd Division.

The 103rd Division spent most of their combat in the Alsace, Rhineland and the Vosges Mountains. There is a book entitled "When the Odds are Even", written by Keith E. Bonn. He tells the entire story of the battle of the Vosges Mountains. In the course of history, no invading army, before us, had ever conquered the rugged mountains.

On March 15th at 7:00 a.m., we were told all the armies would attack the Germans en mass. We took off at exactly 7:00 a.m.—in front of us were smoke screens from our Division, but enemy artillery started coming in. During the course of the fighting I could hardly see the person in front of me. At approximately 7:15 a.m. I heard a strange sound—I hit the ground and got up to find a hole in my left boot. The shrapnel hit my big toe. I wondered around and in the smoke screen without a boot on my left foot for what seemed like an eternity before I found an aid station.

After being treated for my wound I was transferred to the 21st General

Hospital in Nancy, France. I was in the hospital when President Roosevelt died and Ernie Pyle (Dana, Indiana native—Ernie Pyle State Historical Site is 35-40 miles southwest) was killed. Leaving the hospital I was joined by my outfit at Innsbruck, Austria. I was discharged on April 16th, 1946 at Camp Atterbury, Indiana as a T/4.

In Austria I was reassigned to the 434 Chemical 4.2 Mortar Battalion. They were getting us ready for deployment to Japan when the war was announced over.

In November 1945 I was given a 10 day pass to visit Rome, Italy. At the time I was stationed in Innsbruck, Austria. We traveled by rail through the Brenner Pass in the Alps between Austria and Italy. I celebrated New Years Eve on Christmas Eve in 1946.

I was awarded the Purple Heart, Combat Infantry Badge, Bronze Star (without the V), ETO with two clusters, the Good Conduct medal, American Victory Medal and the American Defense Medal.

In August, 1950 I joined the 424 Field Artillery Battalion Reserve Unit knowing it was going to be activated in September. My MOS was a Mess Sgt. On September 15th (the same day that my daughter was born) the 424 was activated. I was sent to Korea for six months of duty then discharged in June 6, 1952.

I want to thank Loran for his story. Loran chose not to go into the gory infantry details. Our area is proud of Loran; he worked tirelessly as the administrator for our Veterans' Administration Regional Office. Loren passed away in 2007. He honorably served (in many different ways) his brother, veterans, of our county for 40 years.

Please note: That he "Pettit" liberated (Feb. 2, 1945) more than a month *after* "XV Corps" (we) had been there!

Also note: The casualties suffered by the VI Corps of the Seventh Army in crossing the Vosges, while (we) "XV Corps" didn't lose a single man!

John (Jack) Eberhardt is showing in this article just *how* history gets distorted.

AFTER WE WENT T THE TIMES, TUESDAY, FEBRUARY 14, 1995 A7

THEN WITHOUT THE LOSS OF A SINGLE MAN

welcome for Princeton 'liberator'

Fifty years after that Feb. 2, 1945, Pettit returned to Colmar — now the borough's sister city — with a group of about 30 Princeton residents. Colmar had been "la poche" — the last remaining pocket of Nazi resistance in France, and its liberation had been especially sweet.

The delegation was unprepared for the warmth of their hosts. "We expected something, but not that amount of enthusiasm," said Claire Byrne. "They were incredible — they treated us as if we have been the liberators."

Pettit had already been on the march a long seven months when he was sent to Colmar. Pettit landed in Normandy in July, a month after D-Day. He paraded with the Allies triumphantly into Paris — and went into combat as soon as he reached the other side, territory still held by the Nazis. After surviving the Battle of the Bulge, Pettit was sent with the small remainder of his division to join the Seventh Army near Colmar.

PETTIT WAS surprised when he saw the Vosges Mountains again, which he had scaled 50 years ago. "I was shocked to see how sheer the mountains were," Pettit said last week. "You say to yourself, how the hell did we get through? The Germans were trapped between Epinal and Colmar. We fought through the mountains, and came right up to the outskirts of Colmar — and they surrendered to the Free French."

Princeton township committee member Phyllis Marchand said that the most moving experience for many was a visit to the American military cemetery up in the Vosges Mountains nearby in Epinal, where

about 5,000 Americans who lost their lives in the battle lay buried.

"It was a misty day," Marchand said, "and as I walked through that scene, with the long lines of crosses and Stars of David — here were all these American men on foreign soil. The caretaker isolated a list of New Jersey men buried there — the list is many pages — and I just started to go through the names. And I felt like I became a mother, a widow, a sister, a grandmother — I became the female survivor."

But the mists of that day cleared into bright sunshine by Saturday, Feb. 4 — the day on which Colmar would celebrate its rebirth. Almost 40,000 people jammed the streets of the town, Princeton Borough Mayor Marvin Reed said, for a parade of French and American military forces, complete with a flyover of French Air Force jets and the entire town decked out in thousands of French, American and other Allied flags.

"I saw Old Glory," said Marchand, "and I turned to someone next to me and , 'You know, the American flag really is distinctive out there. Boy, Betsy Ross sure did a good job.'"

MARCHAND ADDED, "It takes a woman to design that flag!"

But all the appreciation of Americans was not received without a nod to their hosts. In a speech at the ceremony, Reed reminded their hosts that it was following the Battle Of Princeton, during the Revolutionary War, that the French General Lafayette decided to come to America's aid.

On night of Feb. 4, the elegant, gilded Colmar concert hall — more suited to a Mozart string quartet — shook to the sounds of a Glen Miller-style 1940s swing band in a reception attended by the French prime minister, U.S. ambassador Pamela Harriman and many other dignitaries.

Princeton residents said that they will remember many things from their trip. Byrne remembered that any diets in the group fell by the wayside, as they were plied with Alsatian specialities like paté de foie gras and choucroute.

Marchand recalled the hospitality of their hosts, who were so devoted to their guests that she only had the chance to spend $3.93 on the entire trip. "For postcards of the Rue de Marchand," she said.

Courtesy of John S. Eberhardt.

discredit of a valiant foe, but rather to the recognition of the fortitude and determination of Americans trained, motivated and well led, following a well-conceived and executed doctrine.

Seventh U.S. Army, given the mission of driving the Germans from northeastern France in the fall and winter of 1944–45, faced the daunting task of advancing through the Vosges Mountains, an area that, in the history of European warfare, had never been stormed successfully.

From Julius Caesar to Napoleon conquerors avoided or failed to cross the Vosges.

In 1870 the Prussians went around the mountain range, and the Germans practically ignored it in 1941 when they swept to victory. It was the region in which French soldiers held out for five days after their government's capitulation.

The forces engaged in this campaign were remarkably similar. Each had a nucleus of veteran divisions newly strengthened with raw recruits facing their first combat. Each had new divisions that had completed prescribed training programs and were being committed for the final time. Neither side had air support— the Americans because of the weather, the Germans because the Luftwaffe had been, largely, expended. Both had adequate armor but found it difficult to employ it effectively in the mountainous and forested terrain. Both suffered logistics inadequacies, the Americans because they were Gen. Dwight D. Eisenhower's lowest-priority army, the Germans because their war production was being severely restricted. And both, quantitatively, had forces that might have been adequate to the task. Perhaps only psychologically the Americans had an advantage—the Germans, by then, had been losing for almost two years.

From start to finish, it was an infantryman's campaign. It was won by American generalship coupled with a gallant complement of soldiers who almost always killed and captured more than they lost; almost always

achieved their tactical objectives; and almost always survived the rigors, deprivations and horrors of combat better than their opponents.

The book is primarily a scholarly recounting of what was almost a backwater arena of World War II and a campaign that occurred only because of Gen. Eisenhower's "broad front" strategy. In pressing all armies to move relentlessly against the Germans, it is apparent that no thought was given to the impregnability of any piece of terrain, hence Lt. Gen. Alexander M. Patch saluted his boss and got on with the job.

The story is a thorough recounting of the actions of all divisions engaged, spiced with small unit actions of both sides. The tactical decisions and quandaries of commanders are well reported.

As with most such military documentaries, the maps are entirely inadequate for following the text and the

recounting of so many units' activities can become tedious, but most World War II Seventh Army veterans should derive satisfaction that their units are fairly represented in the descriptions of what happened.

In sum, this book is an excellent contribution to military history, a factual accounting of a bit of World War II. It is testimony that when the odds are even, the American soldier is a formidable fighting machine, and accounts to the contrary by some better-known authors are well rebutted. The book also refutes the latter-day contention that Americans engage only in "attrition" warfare, for, from start to finish, the Vosges conquest was a war of planned and executed maneuver by all echelons.

GEN. FREDERICK J. KROESEN, USA Ret., is former commander in chief of U.S. Army Europe and a Senior Fellow of AUSA's Institute of Land Warfare.

Varied Fare

Russia's Arms Catalog, Volume I, Army. *Edited by Nikolai Spassky. Military Parade.* ZigZag Publishing Group, Olympic Tower East, 645 Fifth Ave., New York, NY 10022. 512 pages; photographs; appendices; index; $495.

A reference work providing a unified classifier of the main weapon systems and combat material of the Russian Federation Armed Forces from 1996 to 1997. Especially useful for military and research libraries, the English/Russian language set consists of army, air force, navy, strategic missile forces, air defense, military-space forces and ammunition volumes.

Materials are presented on the basis of the weapon's functional features, and models are classified in terms and codes that are compatible with the Federal Classifier of the United States adopted by NATO.

Volume I, Army, provides approximately 400 armament versions (the bulk of the combat materiel currently in service with the Russian army) and

photographs taken at proving grounds during live firings.

Sections of the volume include ordnance, armor armament and armored materiel, protection facilities, engineer equipment, military motor vehicles, military communications materiel and logistic support technical means.

Volumes II and III are also currently available. Sections of *Volume II, Air Force,* include aircraft, helicopters, simulators, unmanned aircraft systems, guided and unguided weapons, aircraft crew escape equipment and life support equipment. *Volume III, Navy,* includes submarines; surface, support and rescue ships; search, rescue and salvage equipment; coastal defense weapons; ship armament; electronic equipment; ship communication facilities; protection facilities; and engineer support and quartering.

Following the 1997 release of the final four volumes, the set will be updated every two years.

discredit of a valiant foe, but rather to the recognition of the fortitude and determination of Americans trained, motivated and well led, following a well-conceived and executed doctrine.

Seventh U.S. Army, given the mission of driving the Germans from northeastern France in the fall and winter of 1944–45, faced the daunting task of advancing through the Vosges Mountains, an area that, in the history of European warfare, had never been stormed successfully.

From Julius Caesar to Napoleon conquerors avoided or failed to cross the Vosges.

In 1870 the Prussians went around the mountain range, and the Germans practically ignored it in 1941 when they swept to victory. It was the region in which French soldiers held out for five days after their government's capitulation.

The forces engaged in this campaign were remarkably similar. Each had a nucleus of veteran divisions newly strengthened with raw recruits facing their first combat. Each had new divisions that had completed prescribed training programs and were being committed for the final time. Neither side had air support—the Americans because of the weather, the Germans because the Luftwaffe had been, largely, expended. Both had adequate armor but found it difficult to employ it effectively in the mountainous and forested terrain. Both suffered logistics inadequacies, the Americans because they were Gen. Dwight D. Eisenhower's lowest-priority army, the Germans because their war production was being severely restricted. And both, quantitatively, had forces that might have been adequate to the task. Perhaps only psychologically the Americans had an advantage—the Germans, by then, had been losing for almost two years.

From start to finish, it was an infantryman's campaign. It was won by American generalship coupled with a gallant complement of soldiers who almost always killed and captured more than they lost; almost always

achieved their tactical objectives; and almost always survived the rigors, deprivations and horrors of combat better than their opponents.

The book is primarily a scholarly recounting of what was almost a backwater arena of World War II and a campaign that occurred only because of Gen. Eisenhower's "broad front" strategy. In pressing all armies to move relentlessly against the Germans, it is apparent that no thought was given to the impregnability of any piece of terrain, hence Lt. Gen. Alexander M. Patch saluted his boss and got on with the job.

The story is a thorough recounting of the actions of all divisions engaged, spiced with small unit actions of both sides. The tactical decisions and quandaries of commanders are well reported.

As with most such military documentaries, the maps are entirely inadequate for following the text and the

recounting of so many units' activities can become tedious, but most World War II Seventh Army veterans should derive satisfaction that their units are fairly represented in the descriptions of what happened.

In sum, this book is an excellent contribution to military history, a factual accounting of a bit of World War II. It is testimony that when the odds are even, the American soldier is a formidable fighting machine, and accounts to the contrary by some better-known authors are well rebutted. The book also refutes the latter-day contention that Americans engage only in "attrition" warfare, for, from start to finish, the Vosges conquest was a war of planned and executed maneuver by all echelons.

GEN. FREDERICK J. KROESEN, USA Ret., is former commander in chief of U.S. Army Europe and a Senior Fellow of AUSA's Institute of Land Warfare.

French Vets Recall Strasbourg Victory

STRASBOURG, France (AP) — Wearing medals and faded berets, 1,500 veterans of France's famed 2nd Armored Division assembled Sunday to celebrate their liberation of Strasbourg 50 years ago in a lightning assault.

The elderly veterans saluted and sang as city leaders laid a wreath at the monument of Gen. Jacques Leclerc, the commander who led the division in the liberation of Paris in August 1944 and this city on France's eastern edge four months later.

The celebrations are part of five days of ceremonies marking the city's liberation on Nov. 23, 1944.

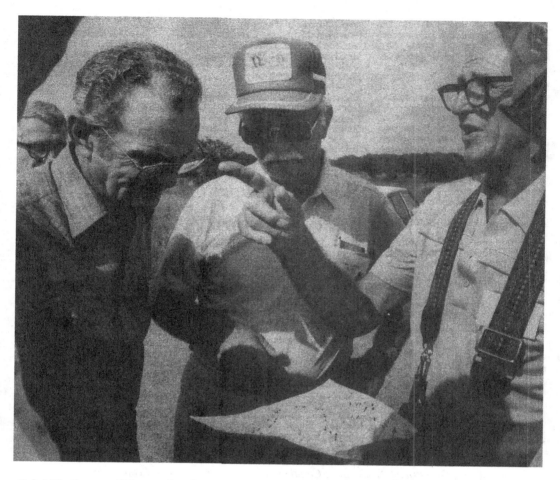

Col. Mike Bavaro of Thousand Oaks, CA, points in the general direction of the barracks where he and his comrades of the 250th FABn stayed when they were stationed at Camp Maxey during World War II. Also shown are Wallace Reid of Grandville, OK, left, and Thomas O. Johnson of Daytona and some of the other men of the 250th during a brief stop at the old camp.

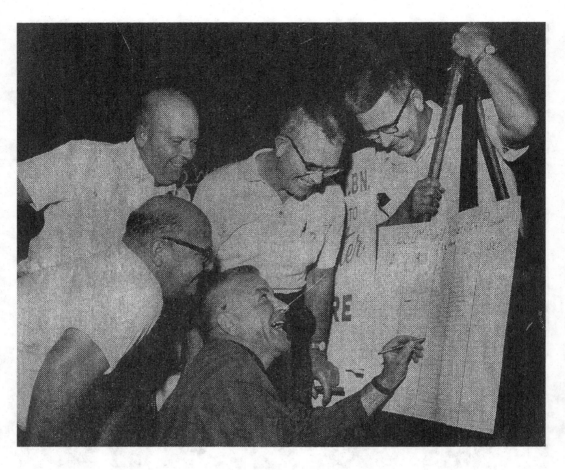

A. Franklin (Tony) Triumpho of Canajoharie, N.Y., signs the 250th Reunion roster. The other happy comrades are, from left, Earl Guidey of Lafayette, LA., Lecile D. Wix of Cullman, AL., Ted Christy of Kingfisher, OK., and A.J. Adair of Enid, OK.

"THIS MUD IS GONNA GET DEEP IF THE WEATHER DOESN'T CHANGE PRETTY SOON!"

—Pfc. Jay Brown

Mrs. Dot Wann sent this cute "cartoon", (top) from the 'Stars & Stripes' dated February 1945

John Wann at Ft. Sill, OK—Sept. 1941 (bottom)

Show horse at Ft. Sill, OK (top)

Training in Horse Drawn
Artillery at Camp Maxey Paris,
Texas, the cavalry component,
mounted originally on horseback,
was being replaced with
motorized armored vehicles
starting in 1941 (bottom)

Wilber D Johnson (top left)

Ural J Isbell & Joe Festervan (top right)

John Wann & Wallace Reid ... best of Friends (bottom)

Ralph Phillips sitting on the wing of a German FW190 (top)

S/Sgt. Cecil Parks made the army his career. Picture Carl Gwin took shows how he wore his cap. (bottom)

Ed Nida, Cecil Parks and Carl Gwin (top)

*Dick Adair, French girl and Orville Shapland...
they gave the little girl the orange (bottom)*

Everett Wheeler in Obermoos,
Austria—June 17, 1945 (top left)

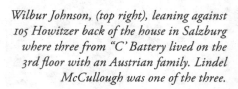

Wilbur Johnson, (top right), leaning against
105 Howitzer back of the house in Salzburg
where three from "C' Battery lived on the
3rd floor with an Austrian family. Lindel
McCullough was one of the three.

A German wrecked AFW surrounded with
stacks of wood ... German defense near
Falaise. It was a climactic battle. (bottom left)

Falaise Pocket littered with equipment and
bodies (bottom right)

Memorial to the meeting
of Polish and American
troops in 1944 that closed
the Falaise Gap stand at
Chambois, France

Ardennes terrain paralleling
ridges and valleys running
NE–SW, forest, swamps,
marshes, and gorges: a deep
narrow pass between steep
heights where rivers and
streams cut through the
long, narrow elevation of
land, hill or mountains.
A very rugged terrain!

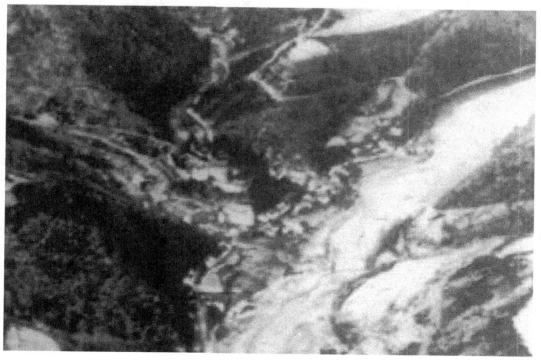

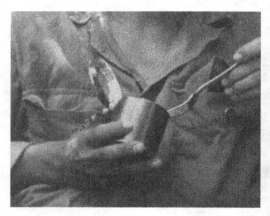

Top left: Ralph Phillips went fishing for some food.

Top right: Thomas Draper and Johnson carrying in their kill and Ken Turner got one that is being carried behind Johnson.

Bottom left: Kenneth Turner front center with mess kit. The K-ration picture is one Carl Gwin had taken & developed himself

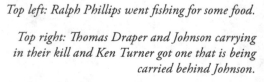

Top: Wilbur D digging a foxhole

Bottom: Jerome Glickman with 50.caliber machine gun

This train at Dachau had 50 railcars containing body remains. (top right)

Pictures Carl Gwin took at Dachau and developed at Salzburg, Austria. After the U.S. Army arrived the prisoners killed the SS guard on the ground. (bottom left and right)

Opposite page bottom right: Eagle's Nest after set afire by SS troops as Allied Forces were moving in.

Opposite page bottom left: Religious cross on a hill above the hotel at Grodig, Austria

German soldier's getting in a German truck, (top right), to surrender as some of the men were going to Hitler's infamous retreat "Eagle's Nest" at Berchtesgaden (top left).

<small>PICTURES: TAKEN BY CARL GWIN</small>

Top: Monte Bankhead wearing his army jacket and holding his framed medals

The 250th Battalion's camp was about in the line area at Salzburg. Salzburg, Austria, a storybook location is located in the beautiful foothills of the Bavarian Alps. It was where the war was announced over on May 8, 1945. It was so peaceful and relaxing, a better place could not have been chosen to be other than HOME.

Salzburg mit Untersberg, Lattengebirge und Reichenhaller Alpen

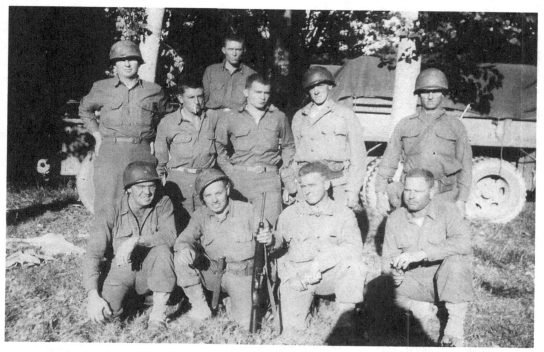

(Top), L–R: James Bailey, Albert Frederick, R L Johnson, Earl McDuffie and Wilbur D Johnson holding gun in background
PICTURES: COURTESY OF WILBUR D JOHNSON—"C" BATTERY MEN

(Bottom), Standing L–R: James Bailey, Albert Frederick, Frank Boyce, Earl McDuffie, Wilbur D Johnson, William Woolsey; Kneeling L–R: Herbert Moyer, Jerome Glickman, R L Johnson and Robert Freasier

Top: L–R: Cox, Chester Blaylock and a fella they called "Bugs". The truck they used from Headquarters' Battery to hauled people from the concentration camp out to the ships and sent home.

Above: Chester Blaylock outside of one of Hitler's guard houses. He had soldiers stationed there to keep the Americans out. This was taken after the war and after Hitler's home had been blown up.

Above: Trucks are from Headquarters' Battery that was loaded with British soldiers. They were being moved to the ships to return home. They had been in the concentration Camp

XV Corps

BATTLES AND CAMPAIGNS

The 250th Field Artillery Battalion: 34 Commanders, Liaison pilots, Surgeon, Officers & etc:

Headquarters Battery: 12 Medics

Headquarters Battery: 111 Enlisted men

"A" Battery 107 Enlisted men

"B" Battery 121 Enlisted men

"C" Battery 104 Enlisted men

Service battery 82 Enlisted men

The 250th served with: 1st, 3rd, and the 7th Armies

Corps: V, VI, XV

Divisions: Armored 2nd French, 12th, 14th, 20th

Divisions: Infantry 3rd, 30th, 35th, 44th, 45th, 63rd, 70th, 80th, 83rd, 90th, 100th

Groups: Cavalry 106th

Groups: FA 173rd, 208th

BATTLES AND CAMPAIGNS

Normandy; Northern France; Rhineland; Central European; Ardennes-Alsace; All members of the 250th earned 5 battle stars, one each for each campaign, plus, arrowhead for amphibious landing. Army of Occupation medal with Germany clasp;

DECORATIONS AND CITATIONS

Eame Theater Ribbon; w-5-1 Silver Star; Bronze Arrowhead; World War II Victory medal lapel button issued ASP September 2, 1945; Good Conduct Ribbon.

250TH FIELD ARTILLERY BATTALION

Honors for outstanding feats, performed during combat in World War II: Brigade Citation by the French Government for going into and taking Strasbourg so fast; highest honor that the French Government bestows on a foreign unit; it entitled each man of the unit to wear the Fourragere of the Croix de Guere.

PRESIDENTIAL CITATION

U.S. Government for meritorious achievement—highest award our government gives to any unit. The 250th Battalion was recognized for being the artillery battalion to fire a round of ammunition across the Rhine River into Germany; Honor given the 250th of firing the 1,000,000 round of ammunition in the VX Corps. On January 29, 1945 at 1430 a brief ceremony was held with generals and colonels present. T.O. Johnson's gun of B-Battery fired the millionth round. Each round of artillery was recorded.

The French Government after 60 years presented each member of the

250th Battalion with a "Thank You America Certificate". Some men were sent the certificate and some were presented personally with the certificate. My husband, Carl, went to Indianapolis, Indiana, where Mr. Dominique Decherf, Consul General of France presented it personally. It was a special day, for three generations of Carl's family were there. It is a rare occasion for three generations to get to witness a piece of *such* history. Our grandson was going to Culver Academy in Culver, Indiana at the time and his Counselor, Major Harris, USMC told Tom to go pay close attention, for it was once in a lifetime thing.

This book provides insight into the strength and courage of a battalion with superior leadership possessed with dignity, optimism and a keen appreciation for each other.

A lot of fighting was done by young boys just out of high school; some not out yet. Too young to realize the true danger, but fought with spirit and a sense of humor through danger. Those fearless moments of danger were intertwined with splashes of long hours of tedious sameness through bombed-out-towns, rugged terrain, and in the worst of weather. Day by day, they slugged it out with grace ... soon had become men.

Memories of General LeClerc with his never ending battle to win against the Boches. General Patton with his full throttle approach—his trades mark!

Generals Patton and Patch both had an outstanding quality—concern for the lives of their soldiers. Patton, older, had been a cavalryman and Patch was an infantryman. They both fought in World War I. General Patch had fought around the Vosges in World War I. He died leaving history as he lived it, *quietly*—never to be truly recognized for the leadership he gave quietly. He never cared for the spotlight as General Patton. His talent did not go unrecognized by the talents of General George C. Marshall. Marshall had General Patch reorganize the Army after the war, with what was called the "Patch Board". The Army today is what General Patch had recommended, but he would never live to see those recommendations implemented. Of course, Gen. Patton is well known. Generals Patton, Patch and LeClerc all died before some of the soldiers returned home. LeClerc died in an airplane crash. Patch of exhaustion, pneumonia and surely a broken heart. He also had been afflicted with malaria. Patton died two weeks after an automobile accident. General Patch lost an only son at Epinal, France. Young Patch was a West Point grad as his father.

General George C. Marshall had been in World War I. In 1939 he was ordained Joint Chief of Staff and, later, became Truman's Secretary of State. He was the first military person to receive the Noble Peace Prize. General Patch commanded the 250th Battalion from September 29, 1944 to the end of the war when General Haislip's was assigned command. Patton's old friend, General Lucian K. Truscott, replaced Patton after General Eisenhower dismissed Patton.

World War I was more of a "cease fire" where World War II was an actual surrender.

General LeClerc, a man of enormous mission, worked well with both the Third and the Seventh Armies. In my research, I have found only the "General Patch's Biography" to give credit to Haislip's XV Corps and General LeClerc's French 2nd Armored Division for the capture of Strasbourg on November 23, 1944.

I found from working with the 250th men what *true* patriotism is. In talking with those I wrote about, I found only a *small* part of their stories came to light and realized they never will completely. For me, to get to compile a book of those small parts was an honor. Although, I wrote sometimes with a little snicker and other times with a lump in my throat and a tear in my eyes, I feel truly blessed. Leaving history for the younger generation and for them to learn what the flag meant to each of these men. Because of their loyalty and dedication is *why* we have the rights we do today. Those sacrifices were made so that our nation may live in freedom. The contributions that our Army, Active, Reserve and National Guard has made for over 232 years has been of tremendous service that cannot be adequately told. Of course, I keep on trying.

A Verse I wrote for "World War II Medic—European Theater" book:

> The silent sound of no artillery left no doubt that the war had come to an End.
>
> Battle hardened soldiers swallowed hard with moist eyes left no doubt that the important mission lay ahead, going Home.
>
> It has been a long, long journey mission no doubt not to be Forgotten.

Ruby M. Gwin